ESL Standards for Pre-K–12 Students

Teachers of English to Speakers of Other Languages, Inc.

Typeset in Berkeley and Franklin Gothic

Printed by Pantagraph Printing, Bloomington, Illinois USA

Teachers of English to Speakers of Other Languages, Inc.
1600 Cameron Street, Suite 300
Alexandria, VA 22314-2751 USA
Tel. 703-836-0774 • Fax 703-836-7864 • E-mail tesol@tesol.edu • http://www.tesol.edu

Project Committee: Deborah Short, Project Director, Center for Applied Linguistics
                       Nancy Cloud, Hofstra University
                       Emily Gómez, Center for Applied Linguistics
                       Else Hamayan, Illinois Resource Center
                       Sarah Hudelson, Arizona State University
                       Jean Ramirez, San Francisco Unified School District

TESOL Board Liaisons: Susan Bayley, Executive Director, TESOL
                       Fred Genesee, University of California, Davis
                       Natalie Kuhlman, San Diego State University
                       Denise Murray, San José State University

Director of Communications and Marketing: Helen Kornblum
Managing Editor: Marilyn Kupetz
Design: Ann Kammerer

Every effort has been made to contact the copyright holders for permission to reprint borrowed material. We regret any oversights that may have occurred and will rectify them in future printings of this work.

TESOL thanks Marjorie Myers, the staff, and students at the Francis Scott Key Elementary School, in Arlington, Virginia, for their participation and assistance. TESOL also appreciates the cooperation of Barbara Jacobson, the staff, and the students at Northern Virginia Community College, Alexandria, Virginia as well as that of Mary Agnes Garman, the staff, and the students at Kings Park Elementary School, Burke, Virginia.

ISBN 0-939791-71-4

Table of Contents

Preface

The *ESL Standards for Pre-K–12 Students* is the result of many years' effort on the part of TESOL members and others who have sought to improve the education of students who are learning English as a second or additional language in the United States. The effort began more than 6 years ago with a TESOL task force chaired by Denise McKeon. It quickly became apparent to ESL educators in the United States at that time that the students we serve were not being included in the standards-setting movement that was sweeping the country. The task force sought to ensure educational equity and opportunity for our students and developed the *Access Brochure,* the text of which can be found in Appendix A. The *Access Brochure* was instrumental in getting school-based personnel to consider our students and include them in school reform efforts.

The task force's goal then shifted, and Else Hamayan became the new chair of a smaller team. Many of the original task force members continued to work on the effort as key advisors and have provided advice and feedback. The goal of this new task force was to create a conceptual framework for setting standards for ESL. *Promising Futures* is the document this team developed, and it is available through TESOL's Professional Paper series. *Promising Futures* is also the basis for the introduction to this standards document.

In March 1995, the TESOL Board of Directors approved a project that would develop a full standards document. The project committee, as the new task force came to be known, created the organization for the current document—establishing the goals, standards, and explications of the standards, namely the descriptors, progress indicators, vignettes, and discussions. We decided to organize the standards by grade-level clusters (pre-K–3, 4–8, 9–12) and to address different English proficiency levels (beginning, intermediate, advanced, and limited formal schooling). Writing teams from many TESOL affiliates, one National Association for Bilingual Education (NABE) affiliate, and several states crafted the standards, descriptors, progress indicators, and vignettes during the summer and fall of 1995. These volunteers drew from their own experiences to create a living document that represents the field of ESL in the United States. A list of these writing team members is found in Appendix B. A draft of the *ESL Standards* was released in March 1996. Since then, numerous educators and policy makers have reviewed the document and commented on it. This final document reflects, to the extent possible, the valuable feedback that TESOL has received.

The project will not finish upon this publication of the *ESL Standards*. TESOL is committed to helping educators translate the goals and standards into classroom practice. Future work includes the preparation of assessment guidelines and scenarios that link these ESL standards with classroom assessments, teacher education and curriculum development materials, and professional development opportunities. In all, this is an exciting effort that should improve the education of students learning English as an additional language and help them achieve success in school and beyond.

Deborah Short
Project Director
March 1997

Introduction: Promising Futures

ESL Standards for Pre-K–12 Students

All elementary and secondary school students currently in the United States will be living in and contributing to an increasingly diverse society and interdependent community of nations in the 21st century. To realize their personal, social, and long-term career goals, individuals will need to be able to communicate with others skillfully, appropriately, and effectively. The challenge of contemporary education is to prepare *all* students for life in this new world, including those learners who enter schools with a language other than English. The purpose of this document is to identify the ESL standards and their role in meeting this challenge.

Why ESL Standards Are Needed

Schools and communities throughout the United States are facing increased linguistic and cultural diversity.

Every year, more and more students who speak languages other than English and who come from homes and communities with diverse histories, traditions, world views, and educational experiences, populate classrooms in urban, suburban, and rural settings. The number of school-age children and youth who speak languages other than English at home increased by 68.6% in the past 10 years. By 1993 English language learners in U.S. public schools numbered more than 2.5 million. Current projections estimate that by the year 2000 the majority of the school-age population in 50 or more major U.S. cities will be from language minority backgrounds.

ESOL students vary greatly in proficiency level and academic needs.

Some ESOL students are recent immigrants, brought to the United States by families seeking refuge from political repression or persecution or by families seeking economic opportunity. Others are members of ethnolinguistic groups that have lived on this continent for generations, some for longer than the United States has existed as a nation. Some have had prior education, including literacy, in their native languages. Others have had limited formal schooling. Some have had normal developmental histories, while others have identified disabilities that challenge their learning. Our primary concerns in this document are with students in elementary and secondary schools who are not native speakers of English, and whom we refer to as ESOL students and learners.

The ESL Standards describe the language skills necessary for social and academic purposes.

The standards described in this document specify the language competencies ESOL students in elementary and secondary schools need to become fully proficient in English, to have unre-

In this document we use two acronyms, ESL and ESOL. ESL refers to the field of English as a second language and to the standards themselves. ESOL (English to speakers of other languages) refers to the learners who are identified as still in the process of acquiring English as an additional language.

stricted access to grade-appropriate instruction in challenging academic subjects, and ultimately to lead rich and productive lives. The development of these standards has been informed by the work of other national standards groups, particularly by the English language arts and foreign language standards. All three language standards projects share an emphasis on the importance of:

- language as communication
- language learning through meaningful and significant use
- the individual and societal value of bi- and multilingualism
- the role of ESOL students' native languages in their English language and general academic development
- cultural, social, and cognitive processes in language and academic development
- assessment that respects language and cultural diversity

The ESL Standards *provide the bridge to general education standards expected of all students in the United States.*

ESL Standards do not and cannot stand alone. Other professional organizations and groups have developed standards that are world-class, important, developmentally appropriate, and useful. These standards mandate high levels of achievement in content learning for all learners, including ESOL students. But the content standards do not provide educators the directions and strategies they need to assist ESOL learners to attain these standards because they assume student understanding of and ability to use English to engage with content. Many of the content standards do not acknowledge the central role of language in the achievement of content. Nor do they highlight the learning styles and particular instructional and assessment needs of learners who are still developing proficiency in English. In sum, the content standards do not address the specific needs of ESOL students who are adding English to their home languages. Therefore, ESL standards are needed.

The ESL standards recognize that upon entry to school ESOL learners must acquire an additional language and culture and learn the English language competencies that are characteristic of native English speakers of the same age and, most importantly, that are fundamental to the full attainment of English language arts and other content standards. The ESL standards articulate the developmental English language needs of ESOL learners and highlight special instructional and assessment considerations that must be given to ESOL learners if they are to benefit from and achieve the high standards proposed for other subjects. Thus, the *ESL Standards* are important because they:

- articulate the English language development needs of ESOL learners
- provide directions to educators on how to meet the needs of ESOL learners
- emphasize the central role of language in the attainment of other standards

The ESL standards articulate the developmental English language needs of ESOL learners and highlight special instructional and assessment considerations that must be given to ESOL learners if they are to benefit from and achieve the high standards proposed for other subjects.

Myths About Second Language Learning

Several myths regarding second language learning prevail both among many lay persons and some educational professionals and policy makers. One intent of this document is to refute these myths.

Myth 1: ESOL students learn English easily and quickly simply by being exposed to and surrounded by native English speakers.

Fact: Learning a second language takes time and significant intellectual effort on the part of the learner. Learning a second language is hard work; even the youngest learners do not simply "pick up" the language.

Myth 2: When ESOL learners are able to converse comfortably in English, they have developed proficiency in the language.

Fact: It can take 6–9 years for ESOL students to achieve the same levels of proficiency in academic English as native speakers. Moreover, ESOL students participating in thoughtfully designed programs of bilingual or sheltered content instruction remain in school longer and attain significantly higher rates of academic achievement in comparison to students without such advantages.

Myth 3: In earlier times immigrant children learned English rapidly and assimilated easily into American life.

Fact: Many immigrant students during the early part of this century did not learn English quickly or well. Many dropped out of school to work in jobs that did not require the kinds of academic achievement and communication skills that substantive employment opportunities require today.

TESOL's Vision of Effective Education for All Students

The role of ESL standards can only be fully understood in the broader context of education for ESOL students. Therefore, before presenting the *ESL Standards,* it is important to describe our overarching vision of effective education.

In TESOL's vision:

- Effective education for ESOL students includes nativelike levels of proficiency in English.
- Effective education for ESOL students includes the maintenance and promotion of ESOL students' native languages in school and community contexts.
- All educational personnel assume responsibility for the education of ESOL students.
- Effective education also calls for comprehensive provision of first-rate services and full access to those services by all students
- Knowledge of more than one language and culture is advantageous for all students.

Effective education for ESOL students includes nativelike levels of proficiency in English.

For ESOL students to be successful in school and ultimately in the world outside school, they must be able to use English to accomplish their academic, personal, and social goals with the same proficiency as native speakers of English. In school environments, ESOL students need to be able to use spoken and written English both to acquire academic content and to demonstrate their learning. ESOL learners also need to be able to follow routine classroom instructions given in English and understand and use appropriate communication patterns so that they can be successful learners in academic environments. Finally, ESOL learners need to use English to function effectively in social settings outside the school, as well as in academic settings. The ESL standards in this document are concerned with these types of social and academic skills. Moreover, appropriate performance and assessment standards that distinguish between language and academic achievement are also required if ESOL students are to be given full credit for learning academic content while acquiring English.

Effective education for ESOL students includes the maintenance and promotion of ESOL students' native languages in school and community contexts.

By definition, ESOL learners already know and use another language. Both the academic achievement and the school completion of ESOL learners is significantly enhanced when they are able to use their native languages to learn in school. In fact, full proficiency in the native language (including literacy) facilitates second language development. Developing and using ESOL students' native languages also serves U.S. national interests because it increases the linguistic and cultural resources available as the United States competes in the global economy. Bilingualism is an asset whose value for the individual and for society can only increase as the U.S. role in the global market place expands in the next century.

All educational personnel assume responsibility for the education of ESOL students.

The attainment of challenging, world-class educational standards by *all* students is only possible if schools design their educational missions with ESOL students, as well as others, in mind. Comprehensive education calls for shared responsibility by and collaboration among all educational professionals working with ESOL students. It also calls for professionals to expand their knowledge to encompass issues of relevance to the education of ESOL students. This expanded knowledge base includes an understanding of similarities and differences in first and second language acquisition, the role of the native language in second language and content learning, instructional methods and strategies that facilitate both English language and content learning, instructional practices that accommodate individual differences in learning styles, the interrelationships between culture, cognition and academic achievement, alternative approaches to assessment, and the importance of community-school linkages in education. These are all part of the professional development of ESL specialists that general educators must tap into if educational reform is to result in the attainment of high standards by all students.

Effective education also calls for comprehensive provision of first-rate services and full access to those services by all students.

Quality educational experiences and services must be made fully accessible to all ESOL students. These include, among others, comprehensive and challenging curricula, access to the full range of curricula (e.g., gifted classes, laboratory sciences, college preparatory courses), safe and

The attainment of challenging, world-class educational standards by *all* students is only possible if schools design their educational missions with ESOL students, as well as others, in mind.

well-equipped classrooms, appropriate instructional practices and assessment measures, inclusion in extracurricular activities, fully and appropriately certified teachers, and other educational specialists and resources. However, this is often not the case in most schools. To have quality programs and to serve ESOL students appropriately on their way to mastery of English, instruction must take into account the different entry-level abilities in English that ESOL learners have. Some learners come to school with oral and written skills; others do not. In addition, where necessary, programs should provide some instruction in the native languages of ESOL students. TESOL's *Access Brochure* provides a description of the conditions needed to provide ESOL students with equitable opportunities to learn. (See Appendix A.)

Knowledge of more than one language and culture is advantageous for all students.

Internationalism is the hallmark of modern U.S. education and of the education reform movement, and linguistic and cultural diversity are the hallmarks of internationalism. The challenge of contemporary education is to contribute to students' abilities to live in increasingly diverse local communities and an ever-shrinking world community. Effective education for the 21st century must provide firsthand opportunities for students to learn about the cultural diversity around them and to learn world languages. Cross-cultural competence can be fostered by meaningful and long-term interactions with others with different world views, life experiences, languages, and cultures. Language learning can be fostered by interactions with native speakers. This means that, not only should ESOL students learn about the U.S. from native-English speakers, but native-English-speaking students, teachers, administrators, and school staff should learn about the world and its languages from ESOL students, their families, and their communities.

Audience

This document is written for educators who work with ESOL learners. First, it is intended for educators who work directly with ESOL students at elementary, middle, and secondary school levels. This includes designated ESL teachers (whether in resource or self-contained settings), bilingual teachers who work with ESOL students in their native languages and English, and teachers who work with ESOL students with special needs and talents. Other educators who will use these standards are content area teachers who teach ESOL students. If ESOL students are to have full access to challenging curricula and to achieve to the same high level in the content areas as native English speakers, then content area specialists must become aware of the importance of language in relationship to their disciplines so that they can better facilitate the academic achievement of their ESOL students.

Curriculum developers and program coordinators are likely to refer to this document as well. The standards and descriptors will be helpful for developers of ESL curricula and may be used to set out learning objectives. The sample progress indicators, vignettes, and discussions offer ideas for learning activities, assessment and program design.

This document may be used as a reference for educators such as counselors, school social workers, and psychologists who provide additional service to ESOL students and for professionals whose activities and decisions affect programs for ESOL students, that is, building

If ESOL students are to have full access to challenging curricula and to achieve to the same high level in the content areas as native English speakers, then content area specialists must become aware of the importance of language in relationship to their disciplines so that they can better facilitate the academic achievement of their ESOL students.

administrators, preservice and in-service teacher educators, and local, state and national policy makers. Parents and communities with ESOL learners may also wish to consult this document so that they may better understand what constitutes appropriate and effective education for their children.

General Principles of Language Acquisition

A number of general principles derived from current research and theory about the nature of language, language learning, human development, and pedagogy, underlie the ESL standards described in this document. These principles are described briefly here.

- ▸ Language is functional.
- ▸ Language varies.
- ▸ Language learning is cultural learning.
- ▸ Language acquisition is a long-term process.
- ▸ Language acquisition occurs through meaningful use and interaction.
- ▸ Language processes develop interdependently.
- ▸ Native language proficiency contributes to second language acquisition.
- ▸ Bilingualism is an individual and societal asset.

Language is functional.

Language, oral and written, is primarily a means of communication used by people in multiple and varied social contexts to express themselves, interact with others, learn about the world, and meet their individual and collective needs. Successful language learning and language teaching emphasize the goal of functional proficiency. This is a departure from traditional pedagogical approaches that view language learning and teaching primarily as mastery of the elements of language, such as grammar and vocabulary, without reference to their functional usefulness. *Therefore, what is most important for ESOL learners is to function effectively in English and through English while learning challenging academic content.*

Language varies.

Language, oral and written, is not monolithic; it comes in different varieties. Language varies according to person, topic, purpose, and situation. Everyone is proficient in more than one of these social varieties of their native language. Language also varies with respect to regional, social class, and ethnic group differences. Such language varieties are characterized by distinctive structural and functional characteristics, and they constitute legitimate and functional systems of communication within their respective sociocultural niches. Additionally, language varies from one academic domain to another—the language of mathematics is different from the language of social studies. As competent language users, ESOL students already use their own language varieties. They must also learn the oral and written language varieties used in schools and in the community in large. What is most important for ESOL learners is to function effectively in academic environments, while retaining their own native language varieties.

Language learning is cultural learning.

Patterns of language usage vary across cultures and reflect differences in values, norms, and beliefs about social roles and relationships in each culture. When children learn their first language, they learn the cultural values, norms, and beliefs that are characteristic of their cultures. To learn another language is to learn new norms, behaviors and beliefs that are appropriate in the new culture, and thus to extend one's sociocultural competence to new environments. To add a new language, therefore, is to add a new culture. Learning a new language and culture also provides insights into one's own language and culture. This is important for ESOL students because general education in U.S. schools tends to reflect a culture other than their own. If ESOL students are to attain the same high standards as native-English-speaking students, educational programs must be based on acknowledgment of, understanding of, respect for, and valuing of diverse cultural backgrounds. What is important for all language learners is to develop attitudes of additive bilingualism and biculturalism.

Language acquisition is a long-term process.

Language acquisition occurs over time with learners moving through developmental stages and gradually growing in proficiency. Individual learners however move through these stages at variable rates. Rates of acquisition are influenced by multiple factors including an individual's educational background, first language background, learning style, cognitive style, motivation, and personality. In addition, sociocultural factors, such as the influence of the English or native language community in the learner's life, may play a role in acquisition. In many instances, learners "pick up" conversation skills related to social language more quickly than they acquire academic language skills. Educational programs must recognize the length of time it takes to acquire the English language skills necessary for success in school. *This means that ESOL learners must be given the time it takes to attain full academic proficiency in English, often from 5 to 7 years.*

> Learners "pick up" conversation skills related to social language more quickly than they acquire academic language skills. Educational programs must recognize the length of time it takes to acquire the English language skills necessary for success in school.

Language acquisition occurs through meaningful use and interaction.

Research in first and second language acquisition indicates that language is learned most effectively when it is used in significant and meaningful situations as learners interact with others (some of whom should be more proficient than the learners are) to accomplish their purposes. Language acquisition takes place as learners engage in activities of a social nature with opportunities to practice language forms for a variety of communicative purposes. Language acquisition also takes place during activities that are of a cognitive or intellectual nature where learners have opportunities to become skilled in using language for reasoning and mastery of challenging new information. *This means that ESOL learners must have multiple opportunities to use English, to interact with others as they study meaningful and intellectually challenging content, and to receive feedback on their language use.*

Language processes develop interdependently.

Traditional distinctions among the processes of reading, listening, writing, and speaking are artificial. So is the conceptualization that language acquisition as linear (with listening preceding speaking, and speaking preceding reading, and so forth). Authentic language often entails the simultaneous use of different language modalities, and acquisition of functional language abilities occurs simultaneously and interdependently, rather than sequentially. Thus, for example, depending on the age of the learner, reading activities may activate the development of speaking abilities, or vice versa. Additionally, listening, speaking, reading, and writing develop as learners engage with and through different modes and technologies, such as computers, music, film, and video. *This means that ESOL learners need learning environments that provide demonstrations of the interdependence of listening, speaking, reading, and writing. They also need to develop all of their language abilities through the use of varied modes and technologies.*

Native language proficiency contributes to second language acquisition.

Because, by definition, ESOL students know and use at least one other language, they have acquired an intuitive understanding of the general structural and functional characteristics of language. They bring this knowledge to the task of second language learning. Some ESOL students also come to the task of learning English and learning content through English already literate in their native languages. These learners know what it means to be literate—they know that they can use written forms of language to learn more about the world, to convey information and receive information from others, to establish and maintain relationships with others, and to explore the perspectives of others. Literacy in the native language correlates positively with the acquisition of literacy in a second language. In addition, academic instruction that includes the use of ESOL students' native languages, especially if they are literate in that language, promotes learners' academic achievement while they are acquiring the English needed to benefit fully from instruction through English. Native language literacy abilities can assist ESOL students in English-medium classrooms to construct meaning from academic materials and experiences in English. And, in learning a new language, students also learn more about their native tongue. *This means that for ESOL learners the most effective environments for second language teaching and learning are those that promote ESOL students' native language and literacy development as a foundation for English language and academic development.*

Bilingualism is an individual and societal asset.

Acquisition of two languages simultaneously is a common and normal developmental phenomenon and that acquisition of a second (or third) language can confer certain cognitive and linguistic advantages on the individual. To realize these benefits, however, advanced levels of proficiency in both languages are necessary. Therefore, the most effective educational environments for ESOL learners are those that promote the continued development of learners' primary languages for both academic and social purposes. In addition, as noted earlier, bilingual proficiency enhances employment possibilities in the international marketplace and enhances the competitive strength of U.S. industry and business worldwide. *This means that bilingualism benefits the individual and serves the national interest, and schools need to promote the retention and development of multiple languages.*

Goals for ESOL Learners

TESOL has established three broad goals for ESOL learners at all age levels, goals that include personal, social, and academic uses of English. Each goal is associated with three distinct standards. In TESOL's vision, ESOL learners will meet these standards as a result of the instruction they receive, thereby achieving the goals. Our schools need to ensure that all students achieve the English language competence needed for academic success and for life in a literate culture.

Goal 1: To use English to communicate in social settings

A primary goal of ESL instruction is to assist students in communicating effectively in English, both in and out of school. Such communication is vital if ESOL learners are to avoid the negative social and economic consequences of low proficiency in English and are to participate as informed participants in our democracy. ESOL learners also need to see that there are personal rewards to be gained from communicating effectively in English. This goal does not suggest, however, that students should lose their native language proficiency.

Standards for Goal 1

Students will:

1. use English to participate in social interaction
2. interact in, through, and with spoken and written English for personal expression and enjoyment
3. use learning strategies to extend their communicative competence

Goal 2: To use English to achieve academically in all content areas

In school settings, English competence is critical for success and expectations for ESOL learners are high. They are expected to learn academic content through the English language and to compete academically with native-English-speaking peers. This process requires that learners use spoken and written English in their schoolwork.

Standards for Goal 2

Students will:

1. use English to interact in the classroom
2. use English to obtain, process, construct, and provide subject matter information in spoken and written form
3. use appropriate learning strategies to construct and apply academic knowledge

Goal 3: To use English in socially and culturally appropriate ways

ESOL students in U.S. schools come into contact with peers and adults who are different from them, linguistically and culturally. The diversity in U.S. schools mirrors the diversity in this country and around the world that young people will encounter as they move into the 21st century world of work. In order to work and live amid diversity, students need to be able to understand and appreciate people who are different and communicate effectively with them. Such communication includes the ability to interact in multiple social settings.

Students will:

1. use the appropriate language variety, register, and genre according to audience, purpose, and setting

2. use nonverbal communication appropriate to audience, purpose, and setting

3. use appropriate learning strategies to extend their sociolinguistic and sociocultural competence

Conclusion

Full proficiency in English is critical for the long-term personal, social, and economic development of all students in the United States. In this document, TESOL outlines a framework for considering and planning language education for ESOL students and for interpreting and making use of the ESL standards. The ESL standards describe the proficiencies in English that ESOL students need to acquire so they can attain the same high level standards in other content domains, including English language arts, as fully proficient English-speaking students. Thus, the *ESL Standards for Pre-K–12 Students* is the starting point for developing effective and equitable education for ESOL students.

Planning effective English language instruction for ESOL students cannot be done in isolation. It must be part of a comprehensive and challenging educational program that takes into account ESOL students' social, educational, and personal backgrounds as well as their existing skills and knowledge bases. It must understand and respond appropriately to the interrelationships between language, academic, and sociocultural development. The linguistic, cognitive, and sociocultural competencies that ESOL students bring to school are a solid base for building their future, in terms of educational and career success. Only if ESL instruction is part of a comprehensive, challenging, and enriching educational program, however, will the promising futures of ESOL learners be realized.

The ESL standards describe the proficiencies in English that ESOL students need to acquire so they can attain the same high level standards in other content domains, including English language arts, as fully proficient English-speaking students.

References for Further Reading

Bilingualism and Second Language Acquisition

August, D., & Hakuta, K. (Ed.). (1997). *Improving schooling for language-minority children: A research agenda.* Washington, DC: National Academy Press.

Bialystok, E., & Hakuta, K. (1994). *In other words: The science and psychology of second-language acquisition.* New York: Basic Books.

Collier, V. (1987). Age and rate of acquisition of second language for academic purposes. *TESOL Quarterly, 21*(3), 617–641.

Collier, V. (1989). How long? A synthesis of research on academic achievement in a second language. *TESOL Quarterly, 23*(2), 509–532.

Hakuta, K. (1986). *Mirror of language: The debate on bilingualism.* New York: Basic Books.

Hoffman, C. (1991). *Introduction to bilingualism.* New York: Longman.

Krashen, S. (1982). *Principles of first and second language acquisition.* Oxford: Pergamon.

Lindfors, J. (1987). *Children's language and learning.* (2nd ed.). Englewood Cliffs, NJ: Prentice-Hall.

McLaughlin, B. (1984). *Second language acquisition in children. Volume 1: Preschool children.* Hillsdale, NJ: Lawrence Erlbaum.

McLaughlin, B. (1985). *Second language acquisition in children. Volume 2: School-age children.* Hillsdale, NJ: Lawrence Erlbaum.

McLaughlin, B. (1992). *Myths and misconceptions about second language learning: What every teacher needs to know.* Educational Practice Report No. 5. Santa Cruz, CA and Washington, DC: National Center for Research on Cultural Diversity and Second Language Learning.

Pease-Alvarez, L., & Hakuta, K. (1992). Enriching our views of bilingualism and bilingual education. *Educational Researcher, 21*(2), 4–6.

Bilingual Education: Importance of Native Language

Collier, V. (1992). A synthesis of studies examining long-term language-minority student data on academic achievement. *Bilingual Research Journal, 16*(1/2), 187–212.

Collier, V. (1995a). Acquiring a second language for school. *Directions in Language and Education 1*(4). Washington, DC: National Clearinghouse for Bilingual Education.

Collier, V. (1995b). *Promoting academic success for ESL students: Understanding second language acquisition for school.* Elizabeth, NJ: New Jersey Teachers of English to Speakers of Other Languages-Bilingual Educators.

Cummins, J. (1981). The role of primary language development in promoting academic success for language minority students. In *Schooling and language minority students: A theoretical framework* (pp. 3–49). Sacramento, CA: California State Department of Education, Division of Instructional Support and Bilingual Education, Office of Bilingual Bicultural Education.

Maez, L., & Gonzalez, G. (1995). Advances in research in bilingual education. *Directions in Language and Education, 1*(5).Washington, DC: National Clearinghouse for Bilingual Education.

McLaughlin, B. (1995). *Fostering second language learning in young children.* Educational Practice Report No. 14. Santa Cruz, CA and Washington, DC: National Center for Research on Cultural Diversity and Second Language Learning.

Ramirez, D., Yuen, S., & Ramey, D. (1991). *Longitudinal study of structured English immersion strategy, early-exit and late-exit transitional bilingual education programs for language-minority children.* San Mateo, CA: Aguirre International.

Ramirez, D. (1992). Executive Summary. *Bilingual Research Journal, 16*(1/2).

Thomas, W., & Collier, V. (1995). Language-minority student achievement and program effectiveness studies support native language development. *NABE News, 18*(8), 5, 12.

United States as a Multilingual Country

Crawford, J. (1992). *Hold your tongue: Bilingualism and the politics of "English only."* Reading, MA: Addison-Wesley.

Crawford, J. (1992). *Language loyalties: A source book on the official English controversy.* Chicago: The University of Chicago Press.

Daniels, H. (Ed.). (1990). *Not only English: Affirming America's multilingual heritage.* Urbana, IL: National Council of Teachers of English.

Effective Education for Language Minority Students

Brinton, D.M., Snow, M.A., & Wesche, M.B. (1989). *Content-based second language instruction.* New York: Newbury House.

Cantoni-Harvey, G. (1987). *Content-area language instruction: Approaches and strategies.* Reading, MA: Addison-Wesley.

Center for Equity and Excellence in Education. (1996). *Promoting excellence: Ensuring academic success for limited English proficient students.* Guiding principles resource guide. Arlington, VA: Author.

Chamot, A.U., & O'Malley, J.M. (1991). *The CALLA handbook.* Reading, MA: Addison-Wesley.

Christian, D. (1995). *Two-way bilingual education: Students learning through two languages.* Educational Practice Report No. 12. Santa Cruz, CA and Washington, DC: National Center for Research on Cultural Diversity and Second Language Learning.

Clegg, J. (Ed.). (1996). *Mainstreaming ESL: Case studies in integrating ESL students into the mainstream curriculum.* Clevedon, England: Multilingual Matters.

Crandall, J.A. (Ed.). (1987). *ESL in content-area instruction.* Englewood Cliffs, NJ: Prentice Hall Regents.

Cummins, J. (1989). *Empowering minority students.* Sacramento, CA: California Association for Bilingual Education.

Curtain, H., & Pesola, C. (Eds.). (1994). *Languages and children: Making the match.* New York: Longman.

Early, M., & Tang, G.M. (1991). Helping ESL students cope with content-based texts. *TESL Canada Journal, 8*(2), 34–45.

Enright, D.S., & McCloskey, M. (1988). *Integrating English: Developing English language and literacy in the multilingual classroom.* Reading, MA: Addison-Wesley.

McKay, S., Faltis, C., & Hudelson, S. (Eds.). (1994). Special-Topic Issue: K–12. *TESOL Quarterly, 28*(3).

Faltis, C. (1993). *Joinfostering: Adapting teaching for the multilingual classroom.* New York: Macmillan.

Freeman, D., & Yvonne, Y. (1994). *Between worlds: Access to second language acquisition.* Portsmouth, NH: Heinemann.

García, E. (1994). *Understanding and meeting the challenge of student cultural diversity.* Boston: Houghton Mifflin.

Genesee, F. (Ed.). (1994). *Educating second language children.* New York: Cambridge.

Genesee, F. (1994). *Integrating language and content: Lessons from immersion.* Santa Cruz, CA and Washington, DC: National Center for Research on Cultural Diversity and Second Language Learning.

Kagan, S. (1986). Cooperative learning and sociocultural factors in schooling. In Bilingual Education Office, California Department of Education (Ed.), *Beyond language: Social and cultural factors in schooling language minority students* (pp. 231–298). Los Angeles: Evaluation, Dissemination and Assessment Center, California State University.

Leone, B., & Cisneros, R. (Eds.). (1995). Special issue on the ESL Component of Bilingual Education in Practice. *Bilingual Research Journal, 19*(3/4).

McKeon, D. (1994). When meeting "common" standards is uncommonly difficult. *Educational Leadership, 42*(8), 45–49.

Mohan, B.A. (1986). *Language and content.* Reading, MA: Addison-Wesley.

National Council of Teachers of Mathematics. (1989). *Curriculum and evaluation standards for school mathematics.* Reston, VA: Author.

Peitzman, F., & Gadda, G. (1994). *With different eyes: Insights into teaching language minority students across the disciplines.* Reading, MA: Addison-Wesley.

Richard-Amato, P.A., & Snow, M.A. (1992). *The multicultural classroom: Readings for content-area teachers.* White Plains, NY: Longman.

Short, D. (1991). *How to integrate language and content instruction: A training manual.* Washington, DC: Center for Applied Linguistics.

Snow, M., Met, M., & Genesee, F. (1989). A conceptual framework for the integration of language and content in second/foreign language instruction. *TESOL Quarterly, 23*(2), 201–217.

Cultural Issues

Flores, J.B. (1996). *Children of la frontera.* Charleston, WV: ERIC Clearinghouse on Rural Education and Small Schools.

Heath, S.B. (1983). *Ways with words: Language, life, and work in communities and classrooms.* Cambridge: Cambridge University Press.

Jacob, E., & Jordan, C. (Eds.). (1993). *Minority education: Anthropological perspectives.* Norwood, NJ: Ablex.

Murray, D. (Ed.). (1992). *Diversity as resource: Redefining cultural literacy.* Alexandria, VA: TESOL.

Nieto, S. (1995). *Affirming diversity: The sociopolitical context of multicultural education.* (2nd ed.). New York: Longman.

Osborne, A.B. (1996). Practice into theory into practice: Culturally relevant pedagogy for students we have marginalized and normalized. *Anthropology and Education Quarterly, 27*(3), 285–314.

Sleeter, C., & Grant, C. (1987). An analysis of multicultural education in the United States. *Harvard Educational Review, 57*(4), 421–444.

Organization of the ESL Standards

The ESL standards have been framed around three goals and nine standards. Each standard is further explicated by descriptors, sample progress indicators, and classroom vignettes with discussions. The standards section of the document that follows is organized into grade-level clusters: pre-K–3, 4–8, and 9–12. Each cluster addresses all goals and standards with descriptors, progress indicators, and vignettes specific to that grade range.

Goals

The goals reflect three overarching areas in which students need to develop competence in English: social language, academic language, and sociocultural knowledge. Each goal is supported by three standards. Upon meeting these standards, students will be proficient in English as a second language.

Standards

The nine content standards indicate more specifically what students should know and be able to do as a result of instruction. The standards in Goal 1 focus on using English to accomplish personal and social interaction tasks. The standards in Goal 2 are concerned with using English to further academic learning and to accomplish academic tasks. The standards in Goal 3 address the cultural parameters of using English with others, including nonverbal communication. The third standard of each goal specifically targets the use of learning strategies to enhance knowledge of the social, academic, and sociocultural purposes of using English. These ESL standards are guidelines that state departments of education and local school districts can use to develop ESL curriculum frameworks.

Descriptors

The descriptors are broad categories of discrete, representative behaviors that students exhibit when they meet a standard. They reflect a range of behaviors across the pre-K–12 spectrum that is needed to use English effectively and accurately in personal, social, and academic circumstances. Although they are not prescriptive, they may assist curriculum developers and classroom teachers in identifying curriculum objectives.

The ESL standards have been framed around three goals and nine standards. Each standard is further explicated by descriptors, sample progress indicators, and classroom vignettes with discussions.

Sample Progress Indicators

The sample progress indicators list assessable, observable activities that students may perform to show progress toward meeting the designated standard. These progress indicators represent a variety of instructional techniques that may be used by teachers to determine how well students are doing and they can be achieved by all students at some level of performance. Because ESOL learners enter school with different levels of English and native language proficiency, the progress indicators represent a sampling of activities that can be demonstrated by the learners at three proficiency levels of English (beginning, intermediate, advanced) and by students with limited formal schooling in their native language. The progress indicators do not evaluate the quality of a student's performance or set benchmarks for reporting that performance. They may assist state and local educators in making those decisions or establishing such benchmarks according to the educational setting, students' backgrounds, goals of instruction, program design, and so forth.

Vignettes

These classroom-based scenes demonstrate the standards in action and describe student and teacher activities that promote English language learning.

The vignettes provide instructional sequences drawn from the real-life experiences of teachers. These classroom-based scenes demonstrate the standards in action and describe student and teacher activities that promote English language learning. All the vignettes, even those concerned with personal language use or cultural interactions, have been situated in schools or similar settings where teachers can monitor the students' proficiency in using or learning to use English for personal, social, and academic purposes.

The vignettes included in this document are intended to be representative of: (a) the types of students for whom these standards are designed in terms of their gender, national origin, and socioeconomic status, as well as their ethnic, linguistic, and educational backgrounds; (b) the types of educational settings in which they are provided ESL instruction; (c) the geographic regions and communities in which they reside in the United States; and (d) the characteristics of teachers who provide ESL instruction in terms of their gender, ethnic, and linguistic backgrounds, professional preparation, and experience.

Although the vignettes are representative of the wide variety of teaching and learning situations in which ESOL learners are placed, each vignette has been written for a particular grade level, type of classroom (e.g., self-contained ESL, transitional bilingual), proficiency level of the students, language of instruction, focus of instruction (e.g., social studies, language arts), and geographic location. Each vignette begins with some background information on the class and concludes with a discussion section.

For the most part, these vignettes depict educational programs for ESOL learners that promote active learning, respect cultural and linguistic diversity, and provide challenging curricula in integrated settings. They represent TESOL's vision for effective education of ESOL learners. However, some vignettes portray more functionally oriented ESL settings for learners with limited educational backgrounds or other learning characteristics that make such programming appropriate. This should not be construed as an endorsement of the "compensatory education" model; rather as with native English speakers, some students will be academically inclined and others may be more vocationally oriented. Overall, the vignettes should be viewed as reflecting quality programs for ESOL learners that are educationally enriching and espouse an additive educational philosophy in which the funds of knowledge that students bring to the classroom are respected and utilized as the foundation for the learning of English and other academic subjects.

Discussions

The discussions connect the vignettes to the standards and selected progress indicators. The discussions explain how the instructional activities described in the vignette encourage students to meet the standard and highlight the students' use of English. Although many of the vignettes apparently describe good teaching practices in general, the discussions make explicit the reasons these practices work well with ESOL learners.

The discussions make explicit the reasons these practices work well with ESOL learners.

Using the ESL Standards

The *ESL Standards* were designed to be useful for teachers and other educators who want to incorporate them in their educational programs for ESOL learners. As educators read through the document, they will recognize that the standards are organized by grade-level clusters, grades pre-K–3, 4–8, and 9–12. The decision to cluster the presentation of the standards, descriptors, progress indicators, vignettes and discussions—despite the wide range of student ages within the clusters—was made for several reasons:

- This grouping of grade levels is similar to the organization of standards in other content areas and thus might facilitate curriculum development, especially when aligning the ESL standards with other academic areas (as anticipated) to help students achieve academically.

- Educators could share ideas across grades within clusters, which may be useful when multiple grades or proficiency levels are placed in one classroom or when local curricula emphasize a topic or language learning activity at a different grade level from the vignette samples listed in this document.

- The three clusters make sense from the perspective of the students' cognitive development and loosely relate to the three common school structures: elementary, middle, and secondary.

- This organization helps build foundational knowledge and increases the sophistication of language use as students move up the grades and get older. In other words, older students are held to higher expectations for demonstrating English proficiency. The descriptors remain the same across the clusters, but more progress indicators are added on at each cluster.

TESOL recognizes that this clustering may be cumbersome for some educators who will need to look across two levels, such as K–5 ESL teachers in elementary schools. To help educators in this regard, the grade-level cluster sections have been assigned tabs, which readers will find in the margins; a matrix at the end of the document cross-references standards, vignettes, and grade levels.

English Language Proficiency Levels

The document also offers variety in its depiction of different English language proficiency levels. Unlike in most other content areas, neither ESL teachers nor ESL curricula can assume that ESOL learners will have similar foundational knowledge based on their grade level.

Whereas a seventh-grade mathematics teacher may reasonably expect a student to have basic knowledge of number theory, operations, fractions, decimals, and percents, which are topics in the K–6 curricula of most schools, ESL teachers cannot assume a seventh-grade ESOL learner has even an intermediate level of English. Therefore, the *ESL Standards* have a more difficult task: not only to show growth in knowledge of the English language across proficiency levels but also to accommodate the language and academic needs of any beginning-level student who might enter the school system at any grade level. This document must reflect that reality and, thus, readers will find classes with beginners at Grade 10 as well as at Grade 1.

To help educators understand the ESL standards that follow, the definitions below explain how the proficiency levels should be interpreted. To simplify the discussion, three general proficiency levels are identified: beginning, intermediate, and advanced, although TESOL acknowledges that some school programs arrange ESOL learners into five levels and others into two. Readers will also notice that the *ESL Standards* recognize that some students enter the U.S. school system with limited formal schooling. This category represents a small but growing number of students in the ESOL population, who increasingly present a challenge for school systems to serve, especially in the secondary grades.

Beginning

At this level, students initially have limited or no understanding of English. They rarely use English for communication. They respond nonverbally to simple commands, statements, and questions. As their oral comprehension increases, they begin to imitate the verbalizations of others by using single words or simple phrases, and begin to use English spontaneously.

At the earliest stage, these learners construct meaning from text primarily through nonprint features (e.g., illustrations, graphs, maps, tables). They gradually construct more meaning from the words themselves, but the construction is often incomplete. They are able to generate simple texts that reflect their knowledge level of syntax. These texts may include a significant amount of nonconventional features, such as invented spelling, some grammatical inaccuracies, pictorial representations, surface features and rhetorical patterns of the native language (i.e., ways of structuring text from native culture and language).

Intermediate

At this level, students understand more complex speech, but still may require some repetition. They acquire a vocabulary of stock words and phrases covering many daily situations. They use English spontaneously, but may have difficulty expressing all their thoughts due to a restricted vocabulary and a limited command of language structure. Students at this level speak in simple sentences, which are comprehensible and appropriate, but which are frequently marked by grammatical errors. They may have some trouble comprehending and producing complex structures and academic language.

Proficiency in reading may vary considerably depending upon the learner's familiarity and prior experience with themes, concepts, genre, characters, and so on. They are most successful constructing meaning from texts for which they have background knowledge upon which to

Using the ESL Standards

build. They are able to generate more complex texts, a wider variety of texts, and more coherent texts than beginners. Texts still have considerable numbers of nonconventional features.

Advanced

At this level, students' language skills are adequate for most day-to-day communication needs. Occasional structural and lexical errors occur. Students may have difficulty understanding and using some idioms, figures of speech, and words with multiple meanings. They communicate in English in new or unfamiliar settings, but have occasional difficulty with complex structures and abstract academic concepts.

Students at this level may read with considerable fluency and are able to locate and identify the specific facts within the text. However, they may not understand texts in which the concepts are presented in a decontextualized manner, the sentence structure is complex, or the vocabulary is abstract. They can read independently, but may have occasional comprehension problems. They produce texts independently for personal and academic purposes. Structures, vocabulary, and overall organization approximate the writing of native speakers of English. However, errors may persist in one or more of these domains.

Students With Limited Formal Schooling

Students with limited formal schooling (LFS) are generally recent arrivals to the United States whose backgrounds differ significantly from the school environment they are entering. This category includes students whose schooling has been interrupted for a variety of reasons, including war, poverty, or patterns of migration, as well as students coming from remote rural settings with little prior opportunity for sequential schooling. These students may exhibit some of the following characteristics:

- pre- or semiliteracy in their native language
- minimal understanding of the function of literacy
- performance significantly below grade level
- a lack of awareness of the organization and culture of school

Although many LFS students are at the beginning level of oral proficiency, some may have reached the intermediate level. Although not fully skilled in the academic domain, these students possess valuable life skills that can serve as a basis for academic learning.

Using the Sample Progress Indicators Across Proficiency Levels

As mentioned earlier, the sample progress indicators are provided to help educators determine how well students are doing. This determination is a local (or state) decision, but the charts on the following pages may guide the understanding of how one progress indicator might be interpreted across grades and English proficiency levels. One chart is presented for

The charts on the following pages may guide the understanding of how one progress indicator might be interpreted across grades and English proficiency levels.

each goal. Each chart focuses on one standard and one progress indicator and complements one of the vignettes from each of the three grade-level clusters.

Brief summary statements of the vignettes are identified in the chart. Whereas the vignettes and discussions that appear in full later in the document might be written for one specific proficiency level and several progress indicators, these reference charts reveal ways that the indicators can be applied to students at different proficiency levels so they can demonstrate some progress toward meeting the standard. The charts indicate, as well, some instructional modifications that might facilitate learning for special needs students.

The charts also represent a process that individual schools and states might want to undertake as they benchmark student learning. Developing charts like these might be akin to designing scoring rubrics for writing assessments, for example.

A thumbnail sketch of how to read the ESL Standards follows the charts. Each component is glossed so that readers can understand at a glance the purpose of the individual components and their importance.

Readers should also be aware that a document on the assessment process is being developed to accompany the *ESL Standards.* The ESL assessment guidelines are being written to help educators:

- understand the purpose and audience of various assessment tools
- plan, collect, analyze and report assessment data
- identify appropriate approaches to assessment with ESOL learners
- connect assessment with the ESL standards

Goal 1, Standard 2

To use English to communicate in social settings:
Students will interact in, through, and with spoken and written English for personal expression and enjoyment

Sample Progress Indicator (SPI): Ask information questions for personal reasons

	Beginning	Intermediate	Advanced	Limited Formal Schooling (LFS)
Grade 2 Vignette Students are in the school library selecting books to take home.	Use simple questions and appropriate gestures to ask the location of certain types of books (e.g., about animals, favorite characters).	Ask "wh" questions about types of books and storylines from peers.	Pose "what if" questions to peers and teacher about alternate endings to stories read.	Use simple, nontechnical words (e.g., *story* for *fiction*) and appropriate gestures to ask the location of certain types of books (e.g., about animals, favorite characters)
Grade 6 Vignette Students find out about heroes for a mural design as part of an after-school art club activity.	In pairs, students ask classmates to name heroes from their countries and describe them orally. May use phrases to make questions.	Ask a friend or teacher a series of simple questions about the life of the hero selected.	Write a series of personal reaction and clarification questions to ask peers after they give oral presentations on a hero.	Using a picture book about a hero, ask questions in native language to learn English vocabulary or in English to confirm words.
Grade 10 Vignette Students participate in an after-school poetry club to read and write poems.	Ask simple questions to generate descriptive terms for use in a poem being written.	Call the local newspaper and ask simple questions concerning guidelines for submitting a poem for competition.	Ask a variety of questions to a poetry club partner to find out what type of poem the partner is writing and how it is progressing.	Use isolated words, phrases and appropriate gestures to ask about timelines for preparing a poem to recite to the group.

Possible learner modifications for exceptional learners include: Behavior management techniques, special student groupings, time extensions for task completion, use of adaptive equipment, paraprofessional support, and materials adaptations (e.g., large-print book).

Goal 2, Standard 2

To use English to achieve academically in all content areas:
Students will use English to obtain, process, construct, and provide subject matter information in spoken and written form

Sample Progress Indicator (SPI): Construct a chart or other graphic showing data

	Beginning	Intermediate	Advanced	Limited Formal Schooling (LFS)
Grade 1 Vignette In math class, students read counting stories, and use unifix cubes to understand basic number theory.	Draw unifix towers in descending order and write the numeral underneath each.	Construct a picture graph illustrating the number of food items that the caterpillar ate and describe the graph orally, using simple sentences.	Draw story board pictures to summarize the plot and include unifix pictures for each food item eaten. Describe storyboard orally or in writing.	Participate in a "physical human chart" that illustrates the number of food items the caterpillar ate in the story, *La Oruga Muy Hambrienta.*
Grades 4–5 Vignette Students read a Native American myth and share myths from their own cultures.	Draw a sequence chart to illustrate the story line of the myth that was read and describe the chart orally, using words and phrases.	Draw a sequence chart to illustrate the story line of the myth that was read and write simple sentences describing the chart.	Develop a comparison chart to compare two nature myths with regard to characters, setting, and conflict resolution.	Make rebus symbols for key vocabulary and then copy part of the myth using rebus symbols for appropriate words.
Grade 11 Vignette Students research a position on the development of a neighborhood toxic waste dump.	Survey neighbors to learn if they are for or against a potential dump site and represent results in a graph.	Illustrate in a chart the advantages and disadvantages of various waste management options.	Using a computer model, generate a graph on the decomposition of different waste material over time and summarize.	Create a photo essay or magazine picture collage to reflect the pros or cons of a dump site and writes captions.

Possible learner modifications for exceptional learners include: Behavior management techniques, special student groupings, time extensions for task completion, use of adaptive equipment, paraprofessional support, and materials adaptations (e.g., large-print book).

Goal 3, Standard 1

To use English in socially and culturally appropriate ways:
Students will use the appropriate language variety, register, and genre according to audience, purpose, and setting

Sample Progress Indicator (SPI): Demonstrate an understanding of ways to give and receive compliments, show gratitude, apologize, express anger or impatience

	Beginning	Intermediate	Advanced	Limited Formal Schooling (LFS)
Grade 3 Vignette Students read and discuss *The Little Red Hen* and reenact part of the story.	Act out a scene from the story in two different ways to show different emotions.	When reading part of the story, explain and justify which emotion is being expressed, orally or in writing.	Write a letter using appropriate form and syntax to one of the characters that the Little Red Hen encountered and explain how she felt.	Act out the sequence of emotions experienced by the Little Red Hen and match the emotions with those listed on word cards.
Grade 7 Vignette Students learn about idioms in context and their appropriate usage.	Identify and explain idioms from the context of a simple dialogue written by classmates.	Write dialogues that incorporate idioms expressing different emotions.	Generate a list of idiomatic expressions and matching non-idiomatic terms and talk about when they are appropriate to use.	Match idioms read aloud to a list of idioms drawn from class research and state which emotion is expressed by each idiom.
Grade 9 Vignette Students learn about returning merchandise to stores through videotaping transactions and analyzing them.	Participate in a role play, returning merchandise and practicing appropriate language in preparation for a real transaction in a store.	Write a letter, with some compound and complex sentences, to a store manager to praise the service of a clerk.	Participate in a conflict resolution role play to mediate between a customer and a security guard, choosing appropriate emotional tone and persuasive language.	Watch videotapes of return transactions and, using symbols, complete a checklist to evaluate appropriate or inappropriate behavior.

Possible learner modifications for exceptional learners include: Behavior management techniques, special student groupings, time extensions for task completion, use of adaptive equipment, paraprofessional support, and materials adaptations (e.g., large-print book).

How to Read the

The top line is the goal and indicates the focus on social or academic language or sociocultural use of language.

Goal 2, Standard 1

To use English to achieve academically in all content areas:
Students will use English to interact in the classroom

The second line is the standard and explains what students should be able to do.

Descriptors

- following oral and written directions, implicit and explicit
- requesting and providing clarification
- participating in full-class, group, and pair discussions
- asking and answering questions
- requesting information and assistance
- negotiating and managing interaction to accomplish tasks
- explaining actions
- elaborating and extending other people's ideas and words
- expressing likes, dislikes, and needs

Sample Progress Indicators

- request supplies to complete an assignment
- use polite forms to negotiate and reach consensus
- follow directions to form groups
- negotiate cooperative roles and task assignments
- take turns when speaking in a group
- modify a statement made by a peer
- paraphrase a teacher's directions orally or in writing
- respond to a teacher's general school-related small talk
- explain the reason for being absent or late to a teacher
- negotiate verbally to identify roles in preparation for a group/class presentation
- ask a teacher to restate or simplify directions
- join in a group response at the appropriate time
- listen to and incorporate a peer's feedback regarding classroom behavior
- greet a teacher when entering class
- distribute and collect classroom materials
- share classroom materials and work successfully with a partner
- ask for assistance with a task

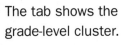

Grades 4–8

The tab shows the grade-level cluster.

ESL Standards for Pre-K–12 Students

83

Descriptors are broad, representative behaviors that students exhibit when they meet a standard.

Progress indicators are assessable, observable activities for students to perform to show progress in meeting the standard.

ESL Standards

Each vignette is based on real classroom scenes. This section explains the grade and student proficiency levels, instructional focus, and location of the school.

4–8 Vignette

Grade Level:	Eighth grade in a sheltered science class
English Proficiency Level:	Variety of levels, high beginning to advanced
Language of Instruction:	English (with 5-minute overviews of activities in Vietnamese and Spanish)
Focus of Instruction:	Science
Location:	Urban school district in the West

Background

The following vignette describes a self-contained, eighth-grade science classroom in an urban school district. The class consists mostly of immigrant students from Vietnam, Central America, and Mexico. All of the students are high beginning- to advanced-level ESL students. The teacher has training and experience working with ESOL students. Two bilingual instructional assistants work in the class on a daily basis. One is a Spanish/English speaker; the other is a Vietnamese/English speaker.

The background section sets the stage for the classroom scene, describing the teacher and students.

Instructional Sequence

Today the class is going to examine containers of various shapes and sizes, hypothesize which ones contain more or less liquid, and then evaluate the capacity of each container. At the beginning of the class, the two assistants provide a 5-minute overview of the day's activity. Then the teacher, using English, demonstrates what the group four glass containers of different shapes and sizes. As she ma language such as, "I think this one will hold less," and "I thin ity." She also uses vocabulary such as, *more, less, most, least, milliliters.* She adds the vocabulary words to a permanent, po demonstration. The teacher then demonstrates how to meas the measure in milliliters, and record the amount in a log. Th orally for the others what each group has to do.

The teacher next divides the class, creating eight groups including as wide a range of English proficiency levels as pos group are instructed to pick up the materials their group will These students check off the materials on their group's mater graduated cylinder, she cannot find one. "Excuse me, Ms. Sn another cylinder?" The teacher directs her to a glass cabinet.

The groups also receive written instructions. The teacher one student read the written directions to make sure that eve teacher and assistants circulate among the groups, clarifying native languages or English as needed. Although the student some initial organization still takes place. In one group, two

84

to record the measurements. Ricardo reminds Rebecca that she was the recorder last time. She concedes and lets U Thi record this time. In another group, Altagracia, an advanced beginner, checks on the directions. "Do we put in water antes de guessing the big ones?" Joel, a high intermediate student, clarifies. "No, we make predictions first. Then we fill them with water."

The groups work on their assignment for the rest of the period, occasionally asking for help from the teacher, one of the instructional assistants, or another group. Near the end of the period, they clean up their supplies and prepare to share their findings with the whole class.

Discussion

Students are encouraged to

- negotiate cooperative roles and task assignments
- paraphrase a teacher's directions orally or in writing
- request supplies to complete an assignment
- ask for assistance with a task

Because of the varying language proficiencies of the students, bilingual instructional assistants are present, and levels of English proficiency are balanced in each group. This both facilitates primary language support for students of lower English proficiency and provides second language support from more fluent peers.

The teacher demonstrates what the students are to do by performing a similar activity. This presentation allows her to pre-teach the vocabulary necessary to understand and discuss the concepts and to complete the tasks. She contextualizes the language, thus making the English comprehensible. The poster-size word bank provides a written version of the words and a handy reference for the students. Less proficient students are able to participate fully in this lesson for two reasons: (a) There is as much primary language support as they need; and (b) the activity involves kinesthetic, hands-on interaction with concrete, demonstrable concepts.

As the students paraphrase the teacher's directions and carry out the activity, they demonstrate that they are able to follow both spoken and written instructions. As needed, they request the necessary supplies to conduct the experiment or help in understanding an aspect of the task from the teacher, assistant, or peer. The students are also able to form groups and negotiate their roles, using appropriate language to do so. These skills will serve them well in most academic settings.

Less proficient students are able to participate fully in this lesson for two reasons: (a) There is as much primary language support as they need; and (b) the activity involves kinesthetic, hands-on interaction with concrete, demonstrable concepts.

85

The instructional sequence describes a brief scene in a lesson that shows the standards in action, organized by grade-level clusters.

The discussion provides a brief explanation of student and teacher actions, linking the vignette to the standard and progress indicators.

Grades Pre-K–3

Diana Wu, Sunana Dhir, and Mohamud Mohamud at Kings Park Elementary School, Burke, Virginia USA.

Grades Pre-K–3

Goal 1, Standard 1

To use English to communicate in social settings:
Students will use English to participate in social interactions

Descriptors

- sharing and requesting information
- expressing needs, feelings, and ideas
- using nonverbal communication in social interactions
- getting personal needs met
- engaging in conversations
- conducting transactions

Sample Progress Indicators

- engage listener's attention verbally or non-verbally
- volunteer information and respond to questions about self and family
- elicit information and ask clarification questions
- clarify and restate information as needed
- describe feelings and emotions after watching a movie
- indicate interests, opinions, or preferences related to class projects
- give and ask for permission
- offer and respond to greetings, compliments, invitations, introductions, and farewells
- negotiate solutions to problems, interpersonal misunderstandings, and disputes
- read and write invitations and thank you letters
- use the telephone

Pre-K–3 Vignette

Grade Level:	First grade in an ESL pull-out class
English Proficiency Level:	Beginning
Language of Instruction:	English
Focus of Instruction:	Language arts
Location:	Suburban school district in the Midwest

Background

The following vignette describes a first-grade, ESL pull-out class in a suburban school district. Ms. López, who is instructing the beginning-level ESOL students, is a bilingual (Spanish/English) teacher certified in elementary education with an ESL credential. The class is multilingual and multiethnic. The students are participating in a prereading activity in preparation for a big book story on farm animals that the entire first-grade class will be reading the following week. Some of the students have had limited formal schooling.

Instructional Sequence

In the ESL room, Ms. López and the beginning ESOL students are reviewing a big book about animals on a farm. Yesterday they worked on animal names, body parts, and counting, using the pictures in the book and small plastic animals. Today, Le comes in with a photo of himself at the park with the ducks. He is excited about sharing his photo with Ms. López and the class. He gets the teacher's attention.

Le:	Teacher, teacher. Look! (He shows the photo to Ms. López.)
Le:	I like ducks.
María:	Ducks at park.
Ms. López:	You saw ducks at the park?
María:	Yes, ducks at the park.
Ms. López:	Did you feed the ducks, give bread to the ducks?
María:	Yes, ducks hungry. I give ducks bread.
Le:	I like to give ducks bread too! They like bread. They eat and eat it all up.
María:	I see baby ducks.
Ms. López:	At the park? You saw baby ducks at the park? How wonderful!
Carlos:	I see baby pigs.
Ms. López:	Where did you see the baby pigs, Carlos?
Carlos:	My uncle's farm.
Ms. López:	Oh, your uncle has a farm. Does he have other animals too?
Carlos:	He has pigs, cows, and a ... how do you say *burro*?
Ms. López:	Oh, he has a donkey.
Carlos:	Donkey.

After a few more children mention farm animals they have seen, Ms. López guides the students to the next activity. She explains they will make a collage of farm animals, using pictures she has cut out of magazines. She shows them a model collage and quickly reviews the names of some of the animals in the artwork. She asks several students to help her distribute supplies.

Chao: (tapping the teacher's shoulder and making a scissors gesture with her hand) Teacher?

Ms. López: Scissors? Do we need scissors?

Chao nods.

Ms. López: No, not today. The pictures are cut out already.

Yoni: Glue please. (He holds out his hand to a child using some glue). I need glue. Give me. (He tries to take it.)

Peter: No, no!

Ms. López: Yoni, Peter is still using the glue. You have to wait. Peter wants you to wait. He can give you the glue when he's finished. (She gestures to Peter.) Peter, when you finish, can you give the glue to Yoni? You can tell Yoni to wait. Just tell him, "Wait."

Peter: Wait.

Yoni: Okay, when you finish, you give me the glue, okay?

Peter: Okay.

The students work on their collages. Ms. López circulates and engages the students in conversation or listens to students interacting. She asks some questions. Some students respond with one word, some respond in their native language, and others use phrases. As the students finish their collages, Ms. López brings them together in the group area. They sit on a rug in a circle. The students talk and show their work. On occasion, Ms. López asks them the name of one of the animals they have chosen or whether they have ever seen one before.

Le holds up his collage to share.

Carlos: Nice picture, Le. You did good.

Ms. López: I think you did very well too, Le.

Le: Thanks.

Chao holds up her collage.

Peter: You have a lot of horses. Do you like horses?

Chao nods and smiles.

Discussion

Students are encouraged to

- engage listener's attention verbally or nonverbally
- volunteer information and respond to questions about self and family
- indicate interests, opinions, or preferences related to class projects
- offer and respond to greetings, compliments, invitations, introductions, and farewells
- negotiate solutions to problems, interpersonal misunderstandings, and disputes

The ESOL students in this class are introduced to concepts in the pull-out ESL class the week before the concepts are introduced in their regular classroom with native and nonnative English speakers. Students use English, their native language, and nonverbal means to participate in the social interactions of a planned activity. During the week of preparation, students learn the names of the animals, talk about their experiences with some of these animals, and apply their knowledge through a hands-on art activity. They express their feelings and communicate their needs with one another and the teacher. They use English and nonverbal means to share classroom materials and to negotiate solutions to disputes. As needed, the teacher models appropriate language, but does not interrupt her students or correct them directly if they make some language errors.

Ms. López creates an environment for social interaction where students are able to use nonverbal means and English to communicate. During the sharing time at the conclusion of the lesson, it is obvious that the students feel comfortable commenting on their classmates' work and asking them questions. The activities have been planned to accommodate a range of proficiency in English, so even Chao, a student with very limited proficiency, is able to get the teacher's attention, communicate her question, and participate in the collage making. The students are also permitted to choose the animals for their collages and later explain their preferences. The form of expression an individual child uses is validated by the teacher as she uses the opportunity to build upon the child's comprehension and expression.

Ms. López creates an environment for social interaction where students are able to use nonverbal means and English to communicate.

Goal 1, Standard 2

To use English to communicate in social settings:
Students will interact in, through, and with spoken and written
English for personal expression and enjoyment

Descriptors

- describing, reading about or participating in a favorite activity
- sharing social and cultural traditions and values
- expressing personal needs, feelings, and ideas
- participating in popular culture

Sample Progress Indicators

- describe favorite storybook characters
- recommend a game, book, or computer program
- listen to, read, watch, and respond to plays, films, stories, books, songs, poems, computer programs, and magazines
- recount events of interest
- ask information questions for personal reasons
- make requests for personal reasons
- express enjoyment while playing a game
- talk about a favorite food or a celebration
- express humor through verbal and non-verbal means

Pre-K–3 Vignette

Grade Level:	Second grade in a transitional bilingual class
English Proficiency Level:	Intermediate
Language of Instruction:	English and Spanish
Focus of Instruction:	Reading
Location:	Urban school district in the Southeast

Background

The following vignette describes a second-grade transitional bilingual class in an urban school district. Ms. Huartado, the certified bilingual teacher, has brought her class to the library to select books and have some free reading time. The students are native Spanish speakers and at an intermediate level in English. Most have been in this school since kindergarten.

Instructional Sequence

It is the middle of the school year and the students are familiar with the library. They enter and begin to look for books to read from the shelves. Mr. Gosler, the librarian, has arranged a special collection of large-print editions of popular stories for one of the students, Dolores, who has a visual impairment. Ms. Huartado had made certain that Dolores wore her corrective lenses when they left the classroom for the library.

Ms. Huartado and Mr. Gosler walk around assisting the children in their book selection. Although Mr. Gosler's use of Spanish is limited, he, like Ms. Huartado, engages the students in discussions about their books in English. Many of the students choose books written in English, such as *Francis the Badger* and *Frog and Toad* stories. A few children prefer books in Spanish. *La Llorona* is a favorite legend.

As Ms. Huartado circulates, she keeps an anecdotal record of the students talking to one another or to Mr. Gosler about their books. Daniela and Sofia look at *Frances the Badger*. Daniela has read it before and she tells Sofia some of the plot. She recommends that Sofia check the book out. Ms. Huartado records the interaction, noting some of the words and phrases, even verb tenses, that Daniela uses as she shares her enthusiasm for the story. A short time later at a reading table, Ms. Huartado listens as Miguel speaks with Mr. Gosler about *Jorge el Curioso en el Zoológico*. Miguel had read the Spanish version of the book but is explaining why he likes Curious George, in English. Miguel uses several adjectives to describe George's behavior, such *clever* and *independent*. He aptly calls George a *troublemaker*. Sometimes, Miguel explains, he gets in trouble like George because he touches or plays with things that he is not supposed to touch.

Discussion

Students are encouraged to

- describe favorite storybook characters
- recommend a book
- recount events of interest

Although this sequence represents library time with a free reading agenda, Ms. Huartado views this trip to the library as an important literacy event. She uses the opportunity to pay attention to how students use English when they are discussing books on their own, rather than in the classroom setting where her presence might influence which students spoke and when. All children are accommodated in the activity by having large-print books available for Dolores and native language books for students who prefer to read in Spanish. Mrs. Huartado keeps an anecdotal record each time the class goes to the library to document the students' words and expressions in order to determine how their use of English is improving. Through this informal manner she can monitor which students have learned to summarize stories, which ones use appropriate adjectives and verbs in retelling, and which ones can justify the recommendations they make to other classmates.

With Mr. Gosler's and Ms. Huartado's presence, students can talk about a story in an extended way to an adult as well as to another student. The second graders do not have to respond to comprehension questions, rather they can guide the conversation as they choose, recounting story events that interest them. Ms. Huartado and Mr. Gosler respond as active conversational partners. Moreover, because Mr. Gosler does not speak much Spanish, the students must rely on their English skills to maintain a conversation with him. Even those students who have read books in Spanish, like Miguel, are encouraged to discuss them in English, recalling the appropriate words and phrases not from the pages of the book, but from their own knowledge of English.

Goal 1, Standard 3

To use English to communicate in social settings:
Students will use learning strategies to extend their
communicative competence

Descriptors

- testing hypotheses about language
- listening to and imitating how others use English
- exploring alternative ways of saying things
- focusing attention selectively
- seeking support and feedback from others
- comparing nonverbal and verbal cues
- self-monitoring and self-evaluating language development
- using the primary language to ask for clarification
- learning and using language "chunks"
- selecting different media to help understand language
- practicing new language
- using context to construct meaning

Sample Progress Indicators

- test appropriate use of new vocabulary, phrases, and structures
- ask someone the meaning of a word
- understand verbal directions by comparing them with nonverbal cues (e.g., folding paper into eighths, lining up)
- tell someone in the native language that a direction given in English was not understood
- recite poems or songs aloud or to oneself
- imitate a classmate's response to a teacher's question or directions
- associate realia or diagrams with written labels to learn vocabulary or construct meaning
- practice recently learned language by teaching a peer

Pre-K–3 Vignette

Grade Level:	Kindergarten in a regular, English language development class
English Proficiency Level:	Variety of levels
Language of Instruction:	English, with some Spanish support
Focus of Instruction:	Free play
Location:	Urban school district in the Southwest

Background

This vignette describes a regular, English language development kindergarten in an urban school district. ESOL and non-ESOL students make up the class, which is taught by Ms. Elkins, a monolingual English speaking teacher, and Mr. Ríos, a Spanish bilingual paraprofessional. Although the majority of ESOL students speak Spanish, there are also speakers of Navajo in this group. Their English proficiency levels vary. During the daily free play period, groups of students participate in one of a variety of student-directed activities, such as community dress-up corner, puzzle construction, and computer games. The teacher explains new play options at the beginning of the week.

Instructional Sequence

Today, William, a high-beginning ESOL student, has chosen the dress-up activity. He would like to be a fireman, but Tracy, a native English speaker, always wants to play that role. William's proficiency in English prevents him from discussing the issue with Tracy, but he remembers that when the teacher wants the children to watch her show them how new equipment works, she always says, "It's my turn." William points to the fireman's outfit and tells Tracy, in a very emphatic tone, "It's my turn." Tracy seems surprised by the self-assuredness of William's request and says, "Okay." Ms. Elkins notices the interaction and notes how important routine language patterns are for ESOL students.

María, an intermediate-level student, wants to play the new computer game. She listened to the teacher's explanation of the directions, but is not sure that she really understands them. She remembers some strategies that Ms. Elkins suggested to use when one does not understand: Observe what her classmates do. Ask another student for help. Or, finally, ask Mr. Ríos or the teacher herself to explain. Because the game is new and no other classmates are at the computer using it, María decides to ask Mr. Ríos for help. She tells Mr. Ríos in Spanish what she remembers and asks for validation and clarification.

Tony, Felipe, and Dora have chosen to reconstruct the giant alphabet floor puzzle. They all intermittently check the wall chart to verify letter order, but Felipe, a transitional-level ESOL student, also continuously chants the alphabet song as he searches for the appropriate letter choice. Mr. Ríos comes over and says to the group, "You are really smart to use the alphabet chart as you complete the puzzle." Felipe looks up and says, "I sing the song too. It helps me find the next letter I need."

Discussion

Students are encouraged to

- test appropriate use of new vocabulary, phrases, and structures
- tell someone in the native language that a direction given in English was not understood
- recite poems or songs aloud or to oneself

In this vignette, three of the children demonstrate their use of learning strategies during the free play period. William hypothesizes that if he uses the teacher's expression, "It's my turn," he will get to use certain materials and other children must wait to use them at a later time. He further hypothesizes that the use of different voice tones will elicit different reactions. He tests these hypotheses on his peer, Tracy, using the language "chunk" and speaking more forcefully. Tracy's response to his strategy validates his hypotheses. Ms. Elkins happens to catch this interaction and records it mentally, recognizing the value of patterned language for beginning-level students.

María is unsure of the accuracy and correctness of what she remembers about the teacher's explanation of the new computer game, so she uses her native language to gain validation from Mr. Ríos. This strategy allows her to monitor and evaluate her understanding and to receive any necessary support. The presence of a Spanish-speaking paraprofessional is helpful for María because she can most accurately demonstrate her current level of understanding in Spanish and receive clarification in the language she knows best. Although the computer game will require that she use English, having the instructions explained in Spanish is most efficient.

Felipe is working on a puzzle with two other classmates. He uses both visual and oral models to guide and verify his choices. He and the others refer to an alphabet chart on the wall and he also sings the alphabet song to help him recall his knowledge of letter order. By using these strategies, he is able to apply learned knowledge to a new activity.

Pre-K–3 Vignette

Grade Level:	Four-year-olds in a regular, preschool class and third grade in a two-way bilingual immersion class
English Proficiency Level:	Newcomer to low intermediate
Language of Instruction:	Spanish and English
Focus of Instruction:	Cross-age activity
Location:	Urban school district in the Midwest

Background

This vignette describes a joint, cross-age activity between a Pre–K Head Start class and a third-grade two-way immersion class. The Head Start class is located in the early childhood center on the same campus as the elementary school. ESOL and non-ESOL students are present in both classes. The two-way class is taught by a bilingual teacher in Spanish and English. The Pre-K class is taught by Mrs. Jenkins, a monolingual English-speaking teacher, with Ms. Díaz, a Spanish-speaking assistant. Mrs. Vásquez, the two-way teacher, is taking the third graders to participate in a Mother's Day/*El Día de la Madre* mini-celebration with the 4-year-old children from the early childhood center.

Instructional Sequence

In preparation for the celebration, the two-way class was instructed on appropriate behavior with preschool children and then role played making new friends. The class also read a big book that the teacher had written about El Día de la Madre. Each student made a Mother's Day card by drawing one scene from the story that he or she liked best on the cover and writing a message inside. The students formed pairs and practiced retelling the story to each other. They would be paired with the 4-year-olds and would tell the story to their partners while referring to the picture on their cards. In their class, the 4-year-olds also talked about making friends with the older students and learned a song, "De colores," that they planned to sing to their new friends.

On the Friday before the Mother's Day holiday, the two classes met on the playing field between the two buildings. To break the ice, the teachers organized a three-legged race so the partners could get to know one another. As the teachers explained how to tie the legs together, William, an ESOL third grader, watched another pair tie up their legs and then worked with Declan, his partner, to do the same.

After playing for a while, all the partners went to sit on blankets that the teachers had spread out on the field. The students had a chance to chat casually, eat some delicious *pan dulce,* and listen as the teachers previewed the schedule. First the third graders would tell the stories and then the preschoolers would sing. As the teachers passed out the cards the third graders had done that referred to the big book, William practiced the story silently. Gabriella, a 4-year-old, started humming "De colores" to herself.

William used his picture while telling the story to Declan. When Declan asked him to explain what one word, *piñata*, meant, William was able to show him a picture of it from his drawing. After 10 minutes of storytelling, the preschoolers gathered together to sing. After several verses, the third graders joined in the refrain. To culminate the day, the teachers and two of the students taught all of the children a dance, *la raspa,* and they took turns trying to break a piñata that Mrs. Vásquez had supplied. Then the children said goodbye to each other and each class went back to its own school.

Discussion

Students are encouraged to

- imitate a classmate's response to a teacher's question or directions
- recite poems or songs aloud or to oneself
- ask someone the meaning of a word
- practice recently learned language by teaching a peer

Students used a number of learning strategies in this vignette to prepare for an encounter with students from another class. The third graders practiced a story in class and created a visual aid to help them recall the story at a later time. William reviewed it to himself before telling it to his partner. The preschoolers also practiced a song in preparation for the Mother's Day celebration. Gabriella hummed the tune before singing it aloud to the third graders. The preschoolers taught the song to the third graders who were able to sing along.

To help understand the teacher's directions for the three-legged race, William observed and mimicked the behavior of his peers. To help his partner learn the meaning of a new word, William referred to his picture of a piñata. All the children listened to the directions and watched the teachers and two students who demonstrated the dance.

Through this cross-age celebration of Mother's Day/El Día de la Madre, the teachers established a setting where the students could make new friends, practice their English language skills, share cultural information, and use learning strategies to promote social conversation with their partners. The teachers made their expectations for student behavior clear before the children met and guided them in enjoyable activities where language could be used naturally.

The teachers made their expectations for student behavior clear before the children met and guided them in enjoyable activities where language could be used naturally.

Goal 2, Standard 1

To use English to achieve academically in all content areas:
Students will use English to interact in the classroom

Descriptors

- following oral and written directions, implicit and explicit
- requesting and providing clarification
- participating in full class, group, and pair discussions
- asking and answering questions
- requesting information and assistance
- negotiating and managing interaction to accomplish tasks
- explaining actions
- elaborating and extending other people's ideas and words
- expressing likes, dislikes, and needs

Sample Progress Indicators

- ask a teacher to restate or simplify directions
- join in a group response at the appropriate time
- listen to and incorporate a peer's feedback regarding classroom behavior
- greet a teacher when entering class
- distribute and collect classroom materials
- share classroom materials and work successfully with a partner
- ask for assistance with a task

Pre-K–3 Vignette

Grade Level:	Kindergarten in a regular class
English Proficiency Level:	Variety of levels
Language of Instruction:	English
Focus of Instruction:	Mathematics
Location:	Urban school district in the Northeast

Background

The following vignette describes a kindergarten class in an urban school district. ESOL and non-ESOL students are present in the class, which is taught by a monolingual English-speaking teacher who is trained to work with ESOL students. The class is multilingual and multiethnic, and the ESOL students have various levels of English language proficiency. Some of them are recent immigrants with no proficiency in English.

Instructional Sequence

Prior to this lesson the children have learned the labels for *circle, square, rectangle,* and *triangle,* and have identified objects in the classroom with these shapes. Today, Mrs. Olson is reading the story, *Friends,* by Alma Flor Ada to her class in a big book format. This is a story of how the little circles, the little rectangles, the little triangles, and the little squares learn how much fun it is to play together. As she reads the story the first time, Mrs. Olson points to the pictures. Then she passes out a large, pre-cut construction paper shape to each student. As she rereads the story, she asks the students to respond by showing their shape and calling out its name as she comes to the appropriate part of the story.

Mrs. Olson asks the children to stand and she leads them in playing "Simon Says" to review the names of the parts of the body, which had been taught previously through songs and stories in other lessons. Mrs. Olson invites the children who are more fluent in English to have a turn being Simon. Then Mrs. Olson asks the children to return to their seats. She holds up samples of large pre-cut shapes that the children will use in making a self portrait. The teacher asks the children, "Which shape will you use to make your head?" as she gestures and points to her own head. Some children respond by pointing to the shape or saying "circle." Mrs. Olson continues by asking the children to show her which shape they might use for the body, the arms, and the legs. She also demonstrates how they will paste the shapes onto a sheet of paper to make their bodies.

Mrs. Olson next calls on several ESOL students to help her pass out materials that the children will need, explaining that she wants each helper to ask, "Do you want some _____?" Four children hand out the shapes; one child hands out paste; one child distributes crayons; one child is in charge of paper; and one child puts yarn of various colors on the worktables. As Lucien puts yarn on one table, Karin asks, "What's that for?" Lucien explains it can be used for hair. "I want brown," replies Karin.

As the children begin to work, Mrs. Olson moves among them. Several children raise their hands to get her attention and ask, "What I do?" " I don't know." "Help me." Other children seek assistance from peers or watch what their friends are doing and take their cues from them. Mrs. Olson repeats the directions for the children who have asked, reinforcing what she means with gestures and the shapes. As the children finish their portraits, Mrs. Olson directs them to write their names on them. She asks several students, including some ESOL learners, to collect the materials that have been used. She reminds the children that they need to ask if the children are done with the materials, not simply take them away. As the helpers collect the materials, Mrs. Olson begins to display the portraits around the room. "I'm not done yet," Julio tells Benyamin as he tries to take the paste. "I must collect it," replies Benyamin. "Wait," says Julio. "Collect the paste at the other tables first. I need one more minute."

Discussion

Students are encouraged to

- ask a teacher to restate or simplify directions
- join in a group response at the appropriate time
- distribute and collect classroom materials
- ask for assistance with a task

Because of the number of ESOL beginners in this class, Mrs. Olson is especially careful to make her input comprehensible. Mrs. Olson uses several routine activities in class and helps the students use routine language patterns for general interactions. In this lesson, she used a big book, a format the children were familiar with. The children could see the pictures as well as hear the story she was reading, and many recited the repeated language expressions.

Mrs. Olson provided the ESOL learners with opportunities to participate in the activities nonverbally as well as verbally and to respond as part of a group rather than responding individually. She accomplished this by giving the children paper shapes to use to indicate that they were following the story. When students recognized the appropriate points in the story to join in, they named the shapes and held them up.

Mrs. Olson paid a lot of attention to classroom routines because she believes understanding and being able to negotiate these routines facilitate learners' success in school. In this lesson, she reminded the students of the type of language to use when involved in routine activities. She also encouraged students to ask for assistance when needed and then she provided it. Mrs. Olson was especially careful to involve the ESOL learners in such activities as distributing and collecting materials. The conversations involving Lucien and Julio, two of the ESOL students, demonstrate their ability to use classroom language and negotiate tasks.

Mrs. Olson paid a lot of attention to classroom routines because she believes understanding and being able to negotiate these routines facilitate learners' success in school.

Goal 2, Standard 2

To use English to achieve academically in all content areas: Students will use English to obtain, process, construct, and provide subject matter information in spoken and written form

Descriptors

- comparing and contrasting information
- persuading, arguing, negotiating, evaluating, and justifying
- listening to, speaking, reading, and writing about subject matter information
- gathering information orally and in writing
- retelling information
- selecting, connecting, and explaining information
- analyzing, synthesizing, and inferring from information
- responding to the work of peers and others
- representing information visually and interpreting information presented visually
- hypothesizing and predicting
- formulating and asking questions
- understanding and producing technical vocabulary and text features according to content area
- demonstrating knowledge through application in a variety of contexts

Sample Progress Indicators

- identify and associate written symbols with words (e.g., written numerals with spoken numbers, the compass rose with directional words)
- define, compare, and classify objects (e.g., according to number, shape, color, size, function, physical characteristics)
- explain change (e.g., growth in plants and animals, in seasons, in self, in characters in literature)
- record observations
- construct a chart or other graphic showing data
- read a story and represent the sequence of events (through pictures, words, music, or drama)
- locate reference material
- generate and ask questions of outside experts (e.g., about their jobs, experiences, interests, qualifications)
- gather and organize the appropriate materials needed to complete a task
- edit and revise own written assignments
- use contextual clues
- consult print and nonprint resources in the native language when needed

Pre-K–3 Vignette

Grade Level:	First grade in a bilingual class
English Proficiency Level:	Mostly beginning, a few intermediate
Language of Instruction:	Spanish and English
Focus of Instruction:	Mathematics
Location:	Suburban school district in the East

Background

The following vignette describes a Spanish/English bilingual first-grade class in a suburban school district. The class consists of mostly immigrant students from the Dominican Republic with a few students of Puerto Rican descent. They are taught by a certified English/Spanish bilingual teacher who is trained to work with ESOL students. Most of the students have a beginning level of proficiency in English, although a few are at a low intermediate level. The students, however, are at different levels of academic (reading and math) readiness. It is early in the school year.

Instructional Sequence

To date, Mr. Quintana has practiced counting with the class as a daily routine, referring to simplified number lines on the desks that the students follow using their fingers. This activity has been extended to counting classroom objects such as desks, chairs, students, rulers, pencils, and so on. The class uses the objects for vocabulary development while learning how to count. In order to strengthen the concept and connection of spoken and written numerals, the results of this daily counting routine have been transcribed often, by using tally marks or numerals on the blackboard, as well as using unifix cubes to represent the objects being counted visually. Several storybooks in English and in Spanish (such as *The Grouchy Ladybug* and *La Oruga Muy Hambrienta*) have been read and reread to the class to introduce counting and measurement with a literature connection.

Today, the class began with a classification activity to introduce the concept of measurement. Students were shown several unifix towers of varying height. The teacher then demonstrated how to organize a sample group from smallest to tallest. Using questions to guide the children, the teacher allowed the students to direct him verbally while arranging the unifix towers according to size. This activity was modeled two more times with individual students acting as teacher while the class provided direction. Then Mr. Quintana used a whole-body activity in which students of varying heights stood in front of class. Through large-group discussion, questions such as: "Who is the smallest?" "Where should he/she stand?" "Who is taller, Mario or Yaritza?" "Where should they stand?" were asked.

Next, the students revisited the activity with the unifix cubes. This time each individual student was given a worksheet that showed several uncolored unifix towers of the exact scale of the actual unifix cubes. The students were then instructed to find the smallest tower on the paper, count, and write the number of cubes underneath. They then verified that it corresponded to the smallest tower that the teacher placed on a table in front of the class. One student volunteered to count the actual tower's cubes so the students could check their work. The students then found the corresponding color among their crayons and colored in the tower. The class continued in this way until each tower was counted and colored.

Then the students cut out the towers to use as manipulatives in classification exercises at their seats as the teacher circulated among students to check for understanding. Next, Mr. Quintana paired the students. Using the student-made unifix paper towers, one student acted as the teacher and placed three or four towers of varying heights in front of the partner. The other student arranged his or her objects accordingly.

For homework, students were asked to draw pictures of their family members according to height, from tallest to shortest.

Discussion

Students are encouraged to

- identify and associate written symbols with words (e.g., written numerals with spoken numbers, the compass rose with directional words)
- define, compare, and classify objects (e.g., according to number, shape, color, size, function, physical characteristics)
- record observations

Mr. Quintana's bilingual first-grade class is composed of nonnative speakers of English. In this vignette the students are using English to reinforce counting and to explore the concept of measurement and classification in their math class. All the students know how to count in Spanish. Here, in this instructional sequence, the students are given the opportunity to learn and practice academic English through verbal communication. The National Council of Teachers of Mathematics (1989) *Curriculum and Evaluation Standards for School Mathematics* suggest that "it is important, therefore, to provide opportunities for [the students] to 'talk mathematics.' Interacting with classmates helps children construct knowledge, learn other ways to think about ideas, and clarify their own thinking" (p. 26).* This instructional sequence provides these opportunities to "talk math" in large-group and small-group activities.

The routines in Mr. Quintana's class reveal a twofold purpose: first, the routines allow beginning-level students to increase their oral comprehension through the use of formulaic phrases; second, the routines build a foundational knowledge of mathematics upon which more complex concepts can be built. This is a helpful process for students who are learning English. Mr. Quintana's careful connection of the spoken and written word, as well as his use of the different systems for writing numbers (e.g., tally marks, numerals) is also important for the bilingual students. Moreover, by using concrete objects the students are familiar with, combined with highly predictable, formulaic utterances, he helps the students recognize the role mathematics has in their lives.

The routines in Mr. Quintana's class reveal a twofold purpose: first, the routines allow beginning-level students to increase their oral comprehension through the use of formulaic phrases; second, the routines build a foundational knowledge of mathematics upon which more complex concepts can be built.

* See References, page 19.

Mr. Quintana allows the students to explore concrete objects and math manipulatives in order to learn basic math concepts. The students begin with a hands-on activity to count and organize cubes in unifix towers. They then proceed to two-dimensional representations of the manipulatives. This vital step helps the students make the connection between the objects that they handled and the objects that they will see on paper in future assignments. At this point they make observations about the number of cubes in the towers and record them. These observations are then checked against the three-dimensional models. Mr. Quintana also teaches them comparative language forms, such as taller, smallest, and so forth.

The home-school connection is strengthened through a follow-up activity in which the heights of family members are compared with each other. Students at all levels of proficiency can draw representations of family members and classify them by size.

Goal 2, Standard 3

To use English to achieve academically in all content areas: Students will use appropriate learning strategies to construct and apply academic knowledge

Descriptors

- focusing attention selectively
- applying basic reading comprehension skills such as skimming, scanning, previewing, and reviewing text
- using context to construct meaning
- taking notes to record important information and aid one's own learning
- applying self-monitoring and self-corrective strategies to build and expand a knowledge base
- determining and establishing the conditions that help one become an effective learner (e.g., when, where, how to study)
- planning how and when to use cognitive strategies and applying them appropriately to a learning task
- actively connecting new information to information previously learned
- evaluating one's own success in a completed learning task
- recognizing the need for and seeking assistance appropriately from others (e.g., teachers, peers, specialists, community members)
- imitating the behaviors of native English speakers to complete tasks successfully
- knowing when to use native language resources (human and material) to promote understanding

Sample Progress Indicators

- use verbal and nonverbal cues to know when to pay attention
- make pictures to check comprehension of a story or process
- scan an entry in a book to locate information for an assignment
- select materials from school resource collections to complete a project
- rehearse and visualize information
- take risks with language
- rephrase, explain, revise, and expand oral or written information to check comprehension
- seek more knowledgeable others with whom to consult to advance understanding
- seek out print and nonprint resources in the native language when needed

Pre-K–3 Vignette

Grade Level:	Kindergarten in a regular class
English Proficiency Level:	High beginning to low intermediate
Language of Instruction:	English
Focus of Instruction:	Language arts
Location:	Suburban school district in the Midwest

Background

The following vignette describes a kindergarten class in a suburban school district. There are ESOL and non-ESOL students in the class, which is taught by a monolingual English-speaking teacher who has not been trained to work with ESOL students. However, she is a veteran kindergarten teacher, has had many ESOL students over the years, and has attended numerous in-service sessions on ESL methods and second language acquisition. She has started team teaching with the ESL teacher once a week because of the larger number of ESOL students that she has in class this year. It is the third quarter of the year and the ESOL students, who represent many language and ethnic backgrounds, have reached a high beginning/low intermediate level of fluency.

Instructional Sequence

The class focuses on one children's book author each month. This month the children are studying Leo Leonni. Mrs. Carroll has read several of Leonni's works to the class. She has also taught them a song, with gestures, about Leo Leonni.

Waldek, who is just beginning to feel comfortable using English words and phrases, has given many signs by his facial expressions and posture that he has been watching and listening attentively to his classmates and the teacher. Today he confidently performs all of the gestures with his classmates and joins in on several phrases of the song which he has mentally rehearsed.

The teacher has read *Swimmy* and is discussing the story and the sequence of events with the children. When asked to tell what they think of Swimmy, Waldek listens to the comments of his classmates, then tentatively raises his hand and volunteers, "He is fish, good fish." "Yes, he is!" Mrs. Carroll responds. Then she asks another child to build on Waldek's answer and to tell what parts of the story show that he is a good fish. Samantha and Jason each give evidence from the story that supports Waldek's conclusion. In the past, Waldek has not felt comfortable volunteering for fear of giving a wrong answer. If he thought his answer might be incorrect, he would break into tears. His growing willingness to volunteer an answer indicates his increasing confidence and comfort in his surroundings.

After further discussion of the book, Mrs. Carroll describes the follow-up art project. Each child will make a fish or sea plant to be part of a class mural about Swimmy in his underwater environment. "Who wants to make Swimmy?" she asks. Buoyed by his earlier success, Waldek volunteers, and his teacher selects him. He confidently returns to his work station to begin his contribution to the project.

He is unable to find the correct color of construction paper, so he goes to the library area of the classroom to get *Swimmy* and takes the book to his teacher. He shows Mrs. Carroll the picture and says, "This paper." She helps him find the right color and names it for him. When he is finished, he proudly pastes his fish in the correct location on the mural, after referring again to the picture in the book. After watching Waldek, some of the other ESOL students review the book as well to check on Swimmy's underwater environment as they prepare their sections of the mural.

Discussion

Students are encouraged to

- ▸ take risks with language
- ▸ select materials from school resource collections to complete a project
- ▸ scan an entry in a book to locate information for an assignment
- ▸ rehearse and visualize information

Waldek, always an attentive student, but initially a reluctant participant in the classroom, displays a growing confidence in functioning in his new language and in the classroom environment. He has watched and imitated his teacher and his classmates intently as they go about the business of learning.

His growing confidence is evident in his volunteering, first to share his perception of Swimmy and then to indicate the contribution he would like to make to the class mural. This volunteering also indicates that he is taking more risks, an important learning strategy for academic success. Waldek's participation in class was also the result of his song rehearsal. By practicing the song mentally, he was able to sing some of the song with his classmates.

When he is able to retrieve the correct book from the classroom library and to request the teacher's help in locating the right color for the construction paper, Waldek shows that he knows how to seek assistance from others and to find and use school resources to complete a project. Other ESOL students also demonstrate their ability to scan for information as they prepare their art assignment.

Mrs. Carroll creates a learning environment that accommodates the limited English proficiency of several of her students. Her teaching strategies allow ESOL learners to participate actively and she demonstrates awareness of the need to accept and expand upon the attempts of students to communicate in their new language. She supports ESOL students in their use of learning strategies, responding to their requests for assistance and aiding them in using classroom resources, which facilitates the students' growth in English and completion of academic tasks.

When he is able to retrieve the correct book from the classroom library and to request the teacher's help in locating the right color for the construction paper, Waldek shows that he knows how to seek assistance from others and to find and use school resources to complete a project.

Goal 3, Standard 1

To use English in socially and culturally appropriate ways:
Students will use the appropriate language variety, register, and
genre according to audience, purpose, and setting

Descriptors

▸ using the appropriate degree of formality with different audiences and settings

▸ recognizing and using standard English and vernacular dialects appropriately

▸ using a variety of writing styles appropriate for different audiences, purposes, and settings

▸ responding to and using slang appropriately

▸ responding to and using idioms appropriately

▸ responding to and using humor appropriately

▸ determining when it is appropriate to use a language other than English

▸ determining appropriate topics for interaction

Sample Progress Indicators

▸ express humor through verbal and non-verbal means

▸ interact with an adult in a formal and informal setting

▸ role play a telephone conversation with an adult

▸ make polite requests

▸ use English and native languages appropriately in a multilingual social situation (e.g., cooperative games or team sports)

▸ write a letter or e-mail message to an adult or a peer using appropriate language forms

▸ demonstrate an understanding of ways to give and receive compliments, show gratitude, apologize, express anger or impatience

▸ greet and take leave appropriately in a variety of settings

Pre-K–3 Vignette

Grade Level:	Third grade in a self-contained ESL class
English Proficiency Level:	Intermediate to advanced
Language of Instruction:	English
Focus of Instruction:	Reading
Location:	Suburban school district in the Northwest

Background

The following vignette describes a third-grade, self-contained ESL classroom in a suburban school district. Ms. Nakamoto is a certified ESL teacher. The 20 students' language backgrounds include Russian, Spanish, Japanese, Korean, Urdu, Gujarati, and Lithuanian. One of these ESL students has learning disabilities. He is served by a resource teacher.

Instructional Sequence

The class has been studying humorous adaptations of folk tales, such as *The True Story of the Three Little Pigs* by Jon Scieszka. Ms. Nakamoto introduces the folk tale, *The Little Red Hen,* and reads the story aloud to the children. A class discussion is conducted about how the animals treated and spoke to one another. Feelings are discussed, and Ms. Nakamoto suggests that the students refer to a chart they developed a few weeks earlier displaying various feelings. The children generate a list of ways to express anger and impatience. Individual students act out one of the ways to express anger while other students guess what is being communicated and suggest things to say that might be more appropriate.

The students are placed in cooperative groups and each group is given a different sequence of events from the story to rewrite, changing the way the little red hen dealt with anger from nonexpression to speaking out to the other animals. One group of students is assigned to come up with a humorous way, another with a very polite way, and another with an inappropriate way. Tamatsu, the student with learning disabilities, is placed in the group that will rewrite the story politely, as his resource room teacher feels that he can then focus on an important social skill simultaneously. She has prepared a guided writing worksheet to aid Tamatsu and his group in rewriting their sequence from the story in a step-by-step fashion to ensure success.

While the students rewrite their sequence, the teacher goes from group to group and assists students in generating language that applies to their task. The students practice acting out their sequence. Afterwards, the whole class acts out the story. Ms. Nakamoto then engages the class in a discussion about what makes the expression of anger humorous, inappropriate, or polite.

Ms. Nakamoto then asks the students to rewrite the story as a whole class and have the animals change their behavior and decide to help the little red hen. In the process, they apologize to her, pay her compliments, and show her their gratitude for baking the bread. During the rewriting procedure, Ms. Nakamoto solicits vocabulary to show gratitude, apology, and appropriate compliments. The students reread the story and illustrate it.

Discussion

Students are encouraged to

- express humor through verbal and nonverbal means
- demonstrate an understanding of ways to give and receive compliments, show gratitude, apologize, express anger or impatience

In this lesson, the teacher introduces the class to adaptations of folk tales, beginning with a humorous rendition of *The Three Little Pigs,* to help the young students understand how language can be selected and changed to reflect different purposes. They discuss the use of language with different emotions and identify ways to express anger and impatience, two emotions that are demonstrated in the story, *The Little Red Hen.* Before the students adapt the story, however, Ms. Nakamoto gives them the opportunity to act out some interactions and discuss appropriate language use as a whole class. A special needs ESL student is fully integrated into the class due to the collaborative efforts of his ESL and resource teachers.

Small groups of students are assigned sequences of the story to rewrite, changing the language according to the prescribed purpose. Students then act out the sequences so the class can see the shift in how the little red hen expresses herself. At the end of the activity, the class creates one final transformation of the story, this time changing the behavior and words of the other animals. Throughout the lesson, Ms. Nakamoto facilitates the students' discussion of language use and acts as a native language informant when necessary.

Goal 3, Standard 2

To use English in socially and culturally appropriate ways: Students will use nonverbal communication appropriate to audience, purpose, and setting

Descriptors

- interpreting and responding appropriately to nonverbal cues and body language
- demonstrating knowledge of acceptable nonverbal classroom behaviors
- using acceptable tone, volume, stress, and intonation, in various social settings*
- recognizing and adjusting behavior in response to nonverbal cues

Sample Progress Indicators

- respond appropriately to a teacher's gesture
- obtain a teacher's attention in an appropriate manner
- use appropriate volume of voice in different settings such as the library, hall, gymnasium, supermarket, and movie theater

* For the purposes of this standard, TESOL considers tone, volume, stress, and intonation as part of nonverbal communication, along with physical manifestations of communication, such as gestures and proxemics.

Pre-K–3 Vignette

Grade Level:	Kindergarten in a two-way bilingual class
English Proficiency Level:	Beginning (for Spanish-speaking students)
Language of Instruction:	Spanish and English
Focus of Instruction:	Science
Location:	Rural school district in the West

Background

In the second week of school, Ms. Piñón prepares the class for their first trip to the science laboratory. For the rest of the year, they will go as a class to Mr. Griffin's science resource room every other week to conduct science experiments. This resource room serves the entire primary school, so the classes take turns. In their regular classrooms, the teachers also teach science concepts and do activities with the students that are integrated with the science lab program.

Instructional Sequence

Although the science resource period will take place during the Spanish portion of the day, Ms. Piñón explains to the students that Mr. Griffin does not speak very much Spanish, so they must try to use English with him. The English-speaking classmates can help out, and she will be in the room too and will help them communicate with Mr. Griffin, if necessary. She asks the kindergartners to line up at the door and walk quietly in the hall. As she opens the door, she hears two students arguing and as she looks back, Ryan shoves José. She raises her two hands, palms pressed together. Clearing her throat to get their attention, she separates her two hands in a gesture she has taught the students to mean they should move away from each other. She then waves her hand at Ryan indicating he should join her in the front of the line. Ryan walks up front while José stays in place.

As the class walks through the hall to the science room, many of the students talk loudly. Ms. Piñón puts her fingers to her lips and they quiet down. They enter the science room and look expectantly at Mr. Griffin. He waves them forward in the room and asks the class to sit in a circle on the rug, while making a circular motion with his hand. He explains they will be studying worms and holds up pictures of worms and a tank with real worms in it as he talks. Teresa yells, "No gusanos! No worms!" Mr. Griffin tells her that she should not yell in class. He then explains that the students do not have to touch the worms today. Ricardo raises his hand and when Mr. Griffin acknowledges him, says, "I touch. I fish." At this point, Ms. Piñón tells Ricardo that she was glad that he raised his hand when he wanted to say something to Mr. Griffin.

Discussion

Students are encouraged to

- obtain a teacher's attention in an appropriate manner
- respond appropriately to a teacher's gesture
- use appropriate volume of voice in different settings such as the library, hall, gymnasium, supermarket, and movie theater

In this vignette, which takes place early in the school year, the kindergarten students learn to respond appropriately to teachers' gestures. Their responses include moving where the teachers indicate and quieting down. Ryan and José correct their behavior according to Ms. Piñón's signals. The students also learn about appropriate volume of voice according to the location where a conversation occurs. Alexis learns not to yell in class and Ricardo demonstrates his understanding of the importance of raising one's hand. While these students are still young and less sophisticated in terms of their own nonverbal communication abilities, they are on the way to understanding what is appropriate for their age and to recognizing physical signals from adults.

While these students are still young and less sophisticated in terms of their own nonverbal communication abilities, they are on the way to understanding what is appropriate for their age and to recognizing physical signals from adults.

Goal 3, Standard 3

To use English in socially and culturally appropriate ways: Students will use appropriate learning strategies to extend their communicative competence

Descriptors

- observing and modeling how others speak and behave in a particular situation or setting
- experimenting with variations of language in social and academic settings
- seeking information about appropriate language use and behavior
- self-monitoring and self-evaluating language use according to setting and audience
- analyzing the social context to determine appropriate language use
- rehearsing variations for language in different social and academic settings
- deciding when use of slang is appropriate

Sample Progress Indicators

- observe language use and behaviors of peers in different settings
- rehearse different ways of speaking according to the formality of the setting
- test appropriate use of newly acquired gestures and language

Pre-K–3 Vignette

Grade Level:	Third grade in a regular class
English Proficiency Level:	Intermediate
Language of Instruction:	English
Focus of Instruction:	Integrated social studies and language arts
Location:	Urban school district in the South

Background

The following vignette describes a third-grade class in an urban school district. The class is taught by Mr. Roberts, a monolingual teacher who has had some training in working with ESOL students. The class is multiethnic and contains non-ESOL and intermediate-level ESOL students. Most of the ESOL students speak Spanish as their first language. The ESOL students have had prior schooling and are literate in their native languages.

Instructional Sequence

The class has been engaged in a thematic unit on Africa and has been discussing the importance of storytelling in certain African cultures. For homework, each student was to have found an idea for a humorous story from something that happened to them or to someone they know well.

Mr. Roberts puts students into cooperative groups, where they take turns telling their humorous stories. After about 15 minutes, Mr. Roberts asks for three volunteers to tell their stories to the entire class. Miguel, Paul, and Sharde volunteer to share theirs while Mr. Roberts makes an audio recording. Sharde's story is particularly engaging—she recalls the previous December, when her baby sister called Santa "an ugly old fella," and she ripped his whole beard right off his face at the mall!

Mr. Roberts asks the whole class to practice telling their stories for homework, and mentions that the principal and some parents will be by tomorrow to listen to some of them. He tells the three volunteers that they will go first tomorrow and that an audiotape will be made of all of the stories.

The next day, Sharde tells her story in front of classmates, parents, and the principal. When she comes to the part about what her sister did to Santa, she says "My sister called Santa an old man and she pulled on his beard. Then it came off."

After the parents and principal leave, Mr. Roberts asks the class if they remember any differences in the way Miguel, Paul, and Sharde told their stories today and the day before. Paul says that Sharde moved her hands around a lot when she told the story to the students, but that she did not motion very much in front of the adults. Mr. Roberts then plays both versions of Sharde's stories and asks for more differences between the two. María notices that Sharde's voice was louder when she told her story just to the students. Eduardo says that Sharde used different words when the principal was in the room. "For example," he says, "she told us that her sister ripped the beard right off the face, but she told the principal in a calmer way, with words like an adult uses."

Discussion

Students are encouraged to

- ▸ rehearse different ways of speaking according to the formality of the setting
- ▸ observe language use and behaviors of peers in different settings

In this assignment, students practice using different language registers in retelling a story. On the first day, students told the stories to their peers, whereas on the second day students told the stories to an audience that included adults. On the second day, Mr. Roberts uses the class discussion and the audiotape comparison to elicit from the students changes that one makes in the language and in the presentation, depending on who is in the audience. Several of Sharde's peers observed changes in her presentation and recalled them for the class.

Sharde is an intermediate-level ESOL student with good oral language skills. She already exhibits a knowledge of language register, as her story's version for the adults is not as exaggerated and she appears more reserved during the delivery. Sharde shows that she is close to reaching the standard; she is aware of language characteristics that are acceptable for peers and ones that are acceptable for adults.

Mr. Roberts has chosen an assignment that the ESOL students can perform successfully. They are able to speak about something from prior knowledge and are given time to practice in front of a small group and at home before performing in front of adults. When Mr. Roberts played back the two versions of Sharde's story, he gave the students who did not remember what they heard another chance to hear the information needed to participate in the class discussion. Finally, through the class discussion, Mr. Roberts was able to distinguish exactly what students change in their language when speaking in different registers.

Sharde shows that she is close to reaching the standard; she is aware of language characteristics that are acceptable for peers and ones that are acceptable for adults.

Grades 4–8

Radhika Katyal, Victor Revollo, and Zuleyma Mendez at the Francis Scott Key Elementary School, in Arlington, Virginia USA.

Goal 1, Standard 1

To use English to communicate in social settings:
Students will use English to participate in social interactions

Descriptors

- ▸ sharing and requesting information
- ▸ expressing needs, feelings, and ideas
- ▸ using nonverbal communication in social interactions
- ▸ getting personal needs met
- ▸ engaging in conversations
- ▸ conducting transactions

Sample Progress Indicators

- ▸ ask peers for their opinions, preferences, and desires
- ▸ correspond with pen pals, English-speaking acquaintances, and friends
- ▸ write personal essays
- ▸ make plans for social engagements
- ▸ shop in a supermarket
- ▸ engage listener's attention verbally or nonverbally
- ▸ volunteer information and respond to questions about self and family
- ▸ elicit information and ask clarification questions
- ▸ clarify and restate information as needed
- ▸ describe feelings and emotions after watching a movie
- ▸ indicate interests, opinions, or preferences related to class projects
- ▸ give and ask for permission
- ▸ offer and respond to greetings, compliments, invitations, introductions, and farewells
- ▸ negotiate solutions to problems, interpersonal misunderstandings, and disputes
- ▸ read and write invitations and thank you letters
- ▸ use the telephone

Grades 4–8

4–8 Vignette

Grade Level:	Fourth grade in a self-contained, content-based ESL class
English Proficiency Level:	Beginning
Language of Instruction:	English
Focus of Instruction:	Social studies
Location:	Urban school district in the Southeast

Background

The following vignette describes a fourth-grade, self-contained ESL class in an urban school district. It takes place in the first month of the school year. The beginning-level, immigrant students are taught by Mr. Thompson, a licensed ESL teacher. Mr. Thompson has observed that his students have limited knowledge of their community. He plans to integrate the teaching of English with an increased awareness of the neighborhood's resources so that students can feel more at home in their neighborhood.

Instructional Sequence

Mr. Thompson begins the lesson by drawing a large, simplified map of the streets and immediate neighborhood around the school on chart paper. Then, in a series of interactions, he elicits the location of the school, using prepositions of place in context. Students take turns coming up to the map in pairs and telling each other how they walk from school to their homes. Where needed, Mr. Thompson provides directional vocabulary for the students as they mark their paths on the map.

Next the teacher models a short dialogue between a person who is lost and a police officer. That person is asking directions to a specific place. He asks the students to practice the conversation in preparation for a role play. Students take turns role playing similar conversations and integrating their own ideas and places of interest. Creativity of expression is encouraged. The "lost" student requests assistance from the "police officer" and on occasion asks for clarification of the directions provided. The teacher models and restates students' words to offer support and guidance.

Students then brainstorm names of community businesses and resources, and Mr. Thompson lists them on the chart. He introduces and reinforces other community vocabulary using pictures, photographs, and student drawings. Students are grouped in fours, with each group divided into two pairs. One pair from each foursome join one of two walking groups that will walk through the school neighborhood.

After careful planning and discussion with students about what to look for, Mr. Thompson and another teacher each take one of the groups on a walk through the school neighborhood. The two groups walk in different directions to cover more territory. The students begin their work by looking for signs to read in English or in other languages. As they walk, the teachers and students point out the location of businesses and community resources, such as the drug store and the post office. Students use a teacher-made trip sheet to tally the number of times they see a particular type of business or resource, discussing along the way the important community resources available to them.

Back in class, pairs reform their groups and discuss what they saw on their separate trips. Then the student groups create a community pictograph on poster paper using the results of their tally. Each group decides on the icons they will use to represent the businesses and community resources they saw. After completing the pictograph, they discuss as a group which business or resource they consider most important in their community. They write some descriptive words, phrases, or sentences on the posters. Each group presents its poster to the class and explains the reasons it chose those icons and that business or resource as most important.

Discussion

Students are encouraged to

- ask peers for their opinions, preferences, and desires
- negotiate solutions to problems, interpersonal misunderstandings, and disputes
- elicit information and ask clarification questions

One of the most difficult social adjustments for immigrant students is to feel oriented to their new country, beginning with their own neighborhood and community. Mr. Thompson aims to make this process take place more smoothly. The map skills portion of his lesson introduces a skill that is especially helpful for beginning-level, immigrant ESOL students.

Mr. Thompson's use of a model conversation based on a real-life situation (being lost, understanding directions given orally) serves two important functions: (a) it helps the students develop language skills for meaningful social interactions, and (b) it aids students in gaining the confidence they will need to ask for clarification or help. The "lost" students had to elicit information from the "police officers" and check their comprehension of the information received. Mr. Thompson also encouraged the students to rely on their own knowledge to create their conversations. Pair work, both during the map activity and the dialogue, provided a support structure for the beginning-level students as well as a genuine conversation partner.

Mr. Thompson often designs his own materials based on his students' unique needs and proficiency levels. In this lesson, he drew a simplified map, collected pictures and photos, and designed a trip tally sheet. This sheet set a purpose for the walk as it helped students focus on desired items. Having two separate groups added another benefit. When they reconvened, the pairs had to use English to explain what they saw. Student interest was further captured as they tallied the types of businesses and community resources they found. The pictograph activity offered the student groups an opportunity to discuss possibilities and negotiate the design of their own icons. In selecting one business or resource to highlight and write about, they also had to use listening, speaking, and negotiating skills.

Grades 4–8

Goal 1, Standard 2

To use English to communicate in social settings:
Students will interact in, through, and with spoken and written
English for personal expression and enjoyment

Descriptors

- describing, reading about, or participating in a favorite activity
- sharing social and cultural traditions and values
- expressing personal needs, feelings, and ideas
- participating in popular culture

Sample Progress Indicators

- recommend a film or videotape to a friend
- write in a diary or personal journal
- describe, read or write about a personal hero
- persuade peers to join in a favorite activity, game, or hobby
- discuss issues of personal importance or value
- locate information for leisure activities (in oral or written form)
- write a poem, short story, play, or song
- describe favorite storybook characters
- recommend a game, book, or computer program
- listen to, read, watch, and respond to plays, films, stories, books, songs, poems, computer programs, and magazines
- recount events of interest
- ask information questions for personal reasons
- make requests for personal reasons
- express enjoyment while playing a game
- talk about a favorite food or a celebration
- express humor through verbal and non-verbal means

Grades 4–8

4–8 Vignette

Grade Level:	Sixth grade in an after-school art program
English Proficiency Level:	Intermediate to advanced
Language of Instruction:	English
Focus of Instruction:	Art
Location:	Suburban school district in the West

Background

The following vignette describes an after-school art program offered to sixth graders at a middle school in a suburban district. Ms. Ashakazian, the art teacher, sponsors the club after school as part of the extended day program. The club includes both native English and nonnative English speakers. The nonnative English speakers come from multiple language backgrounds and study together in the ESL classes at the school.

Instructional Sequence

It is early in the school year and Ms. Ashakazian wants to help the sixth graders feel more at home in their new school. She also knows that many of the students in the art club do not know one another because they recently enrolled from various elementary schools this year. To foster their connection to the middle school and help them get acquainted, she proposes they paint a mural along one of the cafeteria walls. The mural will depict the students' favorite heroes, but the selection of which heroes to paint would be based on a contest. Students would have to research their hero, sketch a mural representation, including a likeness with some symbols, and present a speech nominating their hero. The sixth graders would then vote for the heroes and mural design. The club members are excited about the project and agree to spend about two weeks in preparation before giving their speeches.

The ESOL students tell their ESL teacher, Mrs. Nekola, about the mural contest the next day and request her assistance. She agrees to stay after school for several days to help them with their research and speech writing. When Ms. Ashakazian gives the club members permission to conduct their research in the library, their classrooms, or the art room, some ESOL students join Mrs. Nekola in the classroom to use the computer to search for background information.

Antonio wants to nominate Cesar Chavez, an advocate for the rights of migrant farm workers. Sergei selects Abraham Lincoln as his hero because Lincoln ended slavery. Radika opts for Mahatma Gandhi, her countryman, who preached nonviolent civil disobedience. Mariko proposes Mother Teresa because she helps poor and sick children. As needed, Mrs. Nekola helps the students find information resources on their heroes. She discusses their selections with them, probing why the students find these individuals to be worthy heroes.

After the students conduct their research, they work with the art teacher to design a mural representation. She shows them how to incorporate symbols into their design. In the second week of the project, the sketch is finished and the students ask Mrs. Nekola for help once again. She guides them on the use of persuasive language in their speeches and offers them the chance to practice in front of their peers in class. Each ESOL student who is a member of the art club accepts the challenge and gives the speech in class. The feedback from their peers is useful, especially since it will be their clubmates who will vote for the heroes, not the teacher.

Discussion

Students are encouraged to

- describe, read, or write about a personal hero
- persuade peers to join in a favorite activity, game, or hobby
- listen to, read, watch, and respond to stories, books, and computer programs
- make requests for personal reasons

The art club is a way for students to get together socially and have some fun after school in a supervised way. Students join for their personal enjoyment and artistic interests. ESOL and non-ESOL students mix freely and use English for most of their interactions. The mural painting and hero contest appeal to all the students. Although they conduct some research on their heroes and take some notes, the students do not view this activity as an academic assignment. Several ESOL students request assistance from Mrs. Nekola who is pleased to help. They seek information through various sources—books, computer networks, and individuals. Throughout the course of the project, the students use English in an enjoyable way. Yet, they also learn some speech-making skills and aspects of persuasive rhetoric. They have the opportunity to practice their speeches informally with ESOL classmates before speaking at the club contest.

Goal 1, Standard 3

To use English to communicate in social settings:
Students will use learning strategies to extend
their communicative competence

Descriptors

- testing hypotheses about language
- listening to and imitating how others use English
- exploring alternative ways of saying things
- focusing attention selectively
- seeking support and feedback from others
- comparing nonverbal and verbal cues
- self-monitoring and self-evaluating language development
- using the primary language to ask for clarification
- learning and using language "chunks"
- selecting different media to help understand language
- practicing new language
- using context to construct meaning

Sample Progress Indicators

- use a dictionary to validate choice of language
- ask a classmate whether a particular word or phrase is correct
- use a computer spell checker to verify spelling
- use written sources to discover or check information
- keep individual notes for language learning
- test appropriate use of new vocabulary, phrases, and structures
- ask someone the meaning of a word
- understand verbal directions by comparing them with nonverbal cues (e.g., folding paper into eighths, lining up)
- tell someone in the native language that a direction given in English was not understood
- recite poems or songs aloud
- imitate a classmate's response to a teacher's question or directions
- associate realia or diagrams with written labels to learn vocabulary or construct meaning
- practice recently learned language by teaching a peer

4–8 Vignette

Grade Level:	Seventh grade in a regular class
English Proficiency Level:	Variety of levels
Language of Instruction:	English
Focus of Instruction:	Science
Location:	Urban site in the Northwest

Background

This vignette describes a heterogeneous, seventh-grade, science class in a medium-sized urban school district. ESOL and non-ESOL students are present in the class, which is taught by a teacher bilingual in Spanish and English. ESOL students range from beginning to advanced levels of English proficiency. Mr. Amado, the teacher, is taking the class on a trip to a local science museum.

Instructional Sequence

At the museum, Mr. Amado tells students to pair up. Daniela, a beginning level student, does not know the expression *pair-up,* but she watches the teacher's nonverbal communication and the behavior of other students. She then finds a partner and gets in line.

After an initial introduction to the museum by a guide, the student pairs walk around the exhibits. Yolanda, an advanced beginner, and her partner stop in front of a hands-on science exhibit and look at the written directions and diagrams. Mr. Amado comes by and strategizes with the girls about ways to understand the directions. Using the diagram and guessing at the meaning of some of the technical terms, the girls discuss the directions. When asked, Mr. Amado provides some assistance, but for the most part, the girls take his advice: "Try to figure it out first." Yolanda is finally ready to try the experiment to test the pair's interpretation of the directions. It works.

Another ESOL student pair approaches as Yolanda is finishing the experiment's activities. She tries to explain the directions and the purpose of the experiment to her classmates. As she explains in English, she notices some quizzical looks so she turns to Mr. Amado and asks, "¿Cómo se dice *gear*?" to clarify in Spanish for her peers.

Later, the class eats lunch in the museum cafeteria. Yolanda sees *quiche* on the written menu and asks Mr. Amado, "What's ki-chay?" and points to the word on the menu sign. Mr. Amado says, "Oh, quiche," and Yolanda repeats, "Yes, quiche." Mr. Amado then points to a dish holding a slice of quiche and tells her in Spanish what it is made of. Yolanda repeats to herself, "Quiche, quiche, quiche" while in line. When she gets to the serving counter, she says, "Quiche, please."

Discussion

Students are encouraged to

- understand verbal directions by comparing them with nonverbal cues (e.g., folding paper into eighths, lining up)

- associate realia or diagrams with written labels to learn vocabulary or construct meaning

- practice recently learned language by teaching a peer

- ask someone the meaning of a word

- test appropriate use of new vocabulary, phrases, and structures

In this vignette, low proficiency students such as Daniela watch their teacher's nonverbal cues and the behavior of their classmates to follow the direction to *pair-up*. Their performance of this task demonstrates that they have learned the meaning of this new expression.

At one of the exhibits, Mr. Amado encourages Yolanda to get the meaning of the directions from the context. Yolanda uses the diagram to help understand written directions for carrying out an experiment. She tests her understanding by trying the experiment and sees that it works. She then teaches her knowledge to other classmates, although she asks the teacher for some assistance in order to clarify the meaning of certain words.

Later in the day, Yolanda makes a hypothesis about the pronunciation of *quiche* based on her Spanish literacy. She then checks the meaning by asking her teacher, knowing that this strategy will help her understand the new word so she can learn it. Mr. Amado uses a visual representation, the actual plate of quiche, to explain what quiche is in Spanish and also to model the correct pronunciation in English. Yolanda repeats the word several times to herself to be sure she can recall the English pronunciation and then tests out her newly acquired vocabulary by using it with the cafeteria server.

Yolanda uses the diagram to help understand written directions for carrying out an experiment.

Grades 4–8

Goal 2, Standard 1

To use English to achieve academically in all content areas:
Students will use English to interact in the classroom

Descriptors

- following oral and written directions, implicit and explicit
- requesting and providing clarification
- participating in full-class, group, and pair discussions
- asking and answering questions
- requesting information and assistance
- negotiating and managing interaction to accomplish tasks
- explaining actions
- elaborating and extending other people's ideas and words
- expressing likes, dislikes, and needs

Sample Progress Indicators

- request supplies to complete an assignment
- use polite forms to negotiate and reach consensus
- follow directions to form groups
- negotiate cooperative roles and task assignments
- take turns when speaking in a group
- modify a statement made by a peer
- paraphrase a teacher's directions orally or in writing
- respond to a teacher's general school-related small talk
- explain the reason for being absent or late to a teacher
- negotiate verbally to identify roles in preparation for a group/class presentation
- ask a teacher to restate or simplify directions
- join in a group response at the appropriate time
- listen to and incorporate a peer's feedback regarding classroom behavior
- greet a teacher when entering class
- distribute and collect classroom materials
- share classroom materials and work successfully with a partner
- ask for assistance with a task

4–8 Vignette

Grade Level:	Eighth grade in a sheltered science class
English Proficiency Level:	Variety of levels, high beginning to advanced
Language of Instruction:	English (with 5-minute overviews of activities in Vietnamese and Spanish)
Focus of Instruction:	Science
Location:	Urban school district in the West

Background

The following vignette describes a self-contained, eighth-grade science classroom in an urban school district. The class consists mostly of immigrant students from Vietnam, Central America, and Mexico. All of the students are high beginning- to advanced-level ESL students. The teacher has training and experience working with ESOL students. Two bilingual instructional assistants work in the class on a daily basis. One is a Spanish/English speaker; the other is a Vietnamese/English speaker.

Instructional Sequence

Today the class is going to examine containers of various shapes and sizes, hypothesize which ones contain more or less liquid, and then evaluate the predictions by measuring the capacity of each container. At the beginning of the class, the teacher, Ms. Smith-Sung, and the two assistants provide a 5-minute overview of the day's activities in their respective languages. Then the teacher, using English, demonstrates what the groups are to do by showing the class four glass containers of different shapes and sizes. As she makes her predictions, she models language such as, "I think this one will hold less," and "I think this one has the greatest capacity." She also uses vocabulary such as, *more, less, most, least, equal, amount, capacity, liters,* and *milliliters.* She adds the vocabulary words to a permanent, poster-size wall chart during the demonstration. The teacher then demonstrates how to measure each container's capacity, read the measure in milliliters, and record the amount in a log. Then she asks two students to review orally for the others what each group has to do.

The teacher next divides the class, creating eight groups of four students, with each group including as wide a range of English proficiency levels as possible. Two members from each group are instructed to pick up the materials their group will need to perform the activity. These students check off the materials on their group's materials list. When Tien looks for a graduated cylinder, she cannot find one. "Excuse me, Ms. Smith-Sung," she says. "Where is another cylinder?" The teacher directs her to a glass cabinet. "Thank you."

The groups also receive written instructions. The teacher asks each group to begin by having one student read the written directions to make sure that everyone understands the tasks. The teacher and assistants circulate among the groups, clarifying the instructions in the students' native languages or English as needed. Although the students are used to working in groups, some initial organization still takes place. In one group, two students, Rebecca and U Thi, offer to record the measurements. Ricardo reminds Rebecca that she was the recorder last time. She concedes and lets U Thi record this time. In another group, Altagracia, an advanced beginner, checks on the directions. "Do we put in water antes de guessing the big ones?" Joel, a high intermediate student, clarifies. "No, we make predictions first. Then we fill them with water."

The groups work on their assignment for the rest of the period, occasionally asking for help from the teacher, one of the instructional assistants, or another group. Near the end of the period, they clean up their supplies and prepare to share their findings with the whole class.

Discussion

Students are encouraged to

- negotiate cooperative roles and task assignments
- paraphrase a teacher's directions orally or in writing
- request supplies to complete an assignment
- ask for assistance with a task

Because of the varying language proficiencies of the students, bilingual instructional assistants are present, and levels of English proficiency are balanced in each group. This both facilitates primary language support for students of lower English proficiency and provides second language support from more fluent peers.

The teacher demonstrates what the students are to do by performing a similar activity. This presentation allows her to pre-teach the vocabulary necessary to understand and discuss the concepts and to complete the tasks. She contextualizes the language, thus making the English comprehensible. The poster-size word bank provides a written version of the words and a handy reference for the students. Less proficient students are able to participate fully in this lesson for two reasons: (a) There is as much primary language support as they need; and (b) the activity involves kinesthetic, hands-on interaction with concrete, demonstrable concepts.

As the students paraphrase the teacher's directions and carry out the activity, they demonstrate that they are able to follow both spoken and written instructions. As needed, they request the necessary supplies to conduct the experiment or help in understanding an aspect of the task from the teacher, assistant, or peer. The students are also able to form groups and negotiate their roles, using appropriate language to do so. These skills will serve them well in most academic settings.

Less proficient students are able to participate fully in this lesson for two reasons: (a) There is as much primary language support as they need; and (b) the activity involves kinesthetic, hands-on interaction with concrete, demonstrable concepts.

Grades 4–8

Goal 2, Standard 2

To use English to achieve academically in all content areas: Students will use English to obtain, process, construct, and provide subject matter information in spoken and written form

Descriptors

- comparing and contrasting information

- persuading, arguing, negotiating, evaluating, and justifying

- listening to, speaking, reading, and writing about subject matter information

- gathering information orally and in writing

- retelling information

- selecting, connecting, and explaining information

- analyzing, synthesizing, and inferring from information

- responding to the work of peers and others

- representing information visually and interpreting information presented visually

- hypothesizing and predicting

- formulating and asking questions

- understanding and producing technical vocabulary and text features according to content area

- demonstrating knowledge through application in a variety of contexts

Sample Progress Indicators

- take notes as a teacher presents information or during a film in order to summarize key concepts

- synthesize, analyze, and evaluate information

- write a summary of a book, article, movie, or lecture

- locate information appropriate to an assignment in text or reference materials

- research information on academic topics from multiple sources

- take a position and support it orally or in writing

- construct a chart synthesizing information

- identify and associate written symbols with words (e.g., written numerals with spoken numbers, the compass rose with directional words)

- define, compare, and classify objects (e.g., according to number, shape, color, size, function, physical characteristics)

- explain change (e.g., growth in plants and animals, in seasons, in self, in characters in literature)

- record observations

- construct a chart or other graphic showing data

- read a story and represent the sequence of events (through pictures, words, music, or drama)

- locate reference material

- generate and ask questions of outside experts (e.g., about their jobs, experiences, interests, qualifications)

- gather and organize the appropriate materials needed to complete a task

- edit and revise own written assignments

- use contextual clues

- consult print and nonprint resources in the native language when needed

4–8 Vignette

Grade Level:	Fourth and fifth combined grades in an ESL class
English Proficiency Level:	Mostly high beginning to low intermediate
Language of Instruction:	English
Focus of Instruction:	Language arts
Location:	Urban school district in the Northeast

Background

This vignette describes a combined fourth- and fifth-grade ESL/language arts class that is part of the Spanish and Punjabi bilingual programs in an urban school district. The ESL teacher is monolingual and collaborates with bilingual teachers in planning lessons. The majority of the students are native Spanish speakers, and nine are native Punjabi speakers from India. Most are at the high beginning/low intermediate level, with some recent arrivals from the Dominican Republic. A unit on Native Americans was recently completed, and this follow-up lesson on traditional stories, storytelling, myths, and legends is presented. It is the middle of the school year.

Instructional Sequence

Ms. Johnson introduces the lesson by holding up a picture of a night sky filled with stars. She initiates a class discussion through questions like: "Tell me about this picture." "What do you think of when you see this?" "Have any of you seen a night sky with so many stars?" She gives students time to respond and allows some students to translate for new arrivals.

The teacher next holds up a picture of a coyote, writes *coyote* on the board while saying it, and the class repeats. More discussion about this picture ensues. Students share their knowledge of coyotes and other similar animals. One student from Guatemala describes a time when a coyote rampaged chickens on his uncle's farm. Ms. Johnson affirms the students' responses and explains that this animal is a small wolf. "Besides Guatemala," she asks, "where do you think coyotes live?" Juanita, a beginner, responds, "My country, Mexico." The teacher agrees and adds, "Coyotes usually live in southwestern lands of North America." She uses a map to show the states in the United States where coyotes live and points out Mexico and Guatemala too.

At this point, Eduardo, a special needs student with a behavorial disorder, begins to make loud coyote noises to get attention. Having taught Eduardo in the program for 2 years, Ms. Johnson knows it is best for the class if she ignores his behavior. She moves to another activity and asks the students to recall the land features found in those southwestern areas and has some students draw pictures of the features on the board. She calls on Eduardo to draw a plateau and praises him for his positive contribution. Other students find the symbols on the map that refer to desert and prairie.

The teacher introduces a Native American story, "The Night Sky," by writing the title on the board and explains that it is a myth passed from generation to generation among Native American Indians. Myths often explain how something in nature, like the sun, moon, and stars, came into existence. The teacher explains that Native Americans used animals as heroes who acted in extraordinary or unusual ways, such as creating the sun, moon, and stars. The students are already familiar with vocabulary concepts (e.g., myths, nature, existence) that they studied in their native language.

Ms. Johnson then asks students to share myths from their cultures about animals or nature. One student from the Dominican Republic tells a myth in Spanish to her classmate, who in turn interprets it in English. It is about a man and woman who had a child that they divided into two children by magic. When the children died later in life, their spirits roamed the island seeking to be reunited. Another student shares a myth about an owl, and a third about a tiger in India.

The teacher next directs students to listen and look at the pictures. As she reads the story aloud, she regularly points to the pictures to help with vocabulary and concept development. At times, she writes key words on the board. Afterward, she distributes copies of the story. Student triads read the story together. A strong student is placed in each group to support the oral reading process. Juanita is seated with Sudesh, an intermediate level student from India. Ms. Johnson places Eduardo with these two students who consistently model appropriate classroom behavior and with whom he has worked well before.

Students then retell the story as a class while the teacher records their comments and ideas on the board. As a group, the class reviews the sentences on the board and organizes the story chronologically. Some students recognize gaps and add information. At other points, the teacher asks comprehension questions to elicit more of the plot. She praises the students for their active participation.

As the period draws to a close, the teacher asks the student groups to underline new vocabulary words in the story. These words are shared as a class and one student is selected to add them to the bulletin board word list that is generated with each new thematic unit. For homework, Ms. Johnson assigns the first step of a research project. Students are told to ask their parents, relatives, or neighbors about myths from their native culture that the students will write and illustrate over the next week. The myths will then be published as a class book. Newer students are paired with more capable ones for assistance.

Discussion

Students are encouraged to

- read a story and represent the sequence of events (through pictures, words, music, or drama)
- use contextual clues
- consult print and nonprint resources in the native language when needed
- research information on academic topics from multiple sources

The cooperative setting and peer support aided all levels of proficiency in a comfortable, social atmosphere. The recent arrivals were comfortable questioning and sharing ideas with classmates who spoke their native language. Their cognitive abilities were not curtailed because they were able to think and express themselves in their native language if necessary, yet they witnessed their ideas being transformed into English. The teacher's use of nonverbal pictorial cues enabled all students either to connect with their own background schema or associate the visual concepts to the printed words and phrases.

The collaborative efforts of the ESL and bilingual teachers reinforced the Native American theme and also aided in the students' cognitive development. Through collaboration across the ESL and bilingual classrooms, the students became familiar with new concepts prior to the actual lesson. This created a pleasant environment and lessened anxiety levels.

The teacher recognized and was comfortable with the need for some students to speak in their native language as an intermediary step to becoming more proficient in English.

In previewing the story, the teacher used pictures and words written on the board to prepare the students for the reading. Encouraging the students to tell myths from their culture demonstrated her interest and respect for their heritage. The teacher recognized and was comfortable with the need for some students to speak in their native language as an intermediary step to becoming more proficient in English. She effectively included a student with a behavioral disorder in the lesson through positive reinforcement, selective attention, careful grouping, and peer modeling techniques. Ms. Johnson also linked the setting of the story with social studies concepts (i.e., land features, map legends) that the students had already studied and used this occasion to review some of them. Throughout this prereading phase, students were able to verbalize their prior knowledge and make connections to the new lesson. This preview activity helped the students get more meaning from context as they read the story later.

The teacher's oral presentation of the story provided a language model for the students. The group activity gave all students practice reading aloud with peer support and also helped develop their pronunciation skills. The retelling activity provided more reinforcement of the connection between the written and spoken word while at the same time establishing a common academic task, sequencing a story. The vocabulary activity was another cooperative task that benefited the bilingual students.

Finally, the creation of the class book of legends and myths will enable the students to relate their cultures with the Native American Indians'. They will involve their family network to research their project which will foster the home-school connection. The beginning-level students will be paired to write their stories, perhaps relating them in their native language and then having their partner translate the stories into English. In both of these activities, the ESOL students will be assisted by more knowledgeable others and be able to work with nonprint as well as print sources to complete their task.

Goal 2, Standard 3

To use English to achieve academically in all content areas:
Students will use appropriate learning strategies to construct and
apply academic knowledge

Descriptors

- focusing attention selectively
- applying basic reading comprehension skills such as skimming, scanning, previewing, and reviewing text
- using context to construct meaning
- taking notes to record important information and aid one's own learning
- applying self-monitoring and self-corrective strategies to build and expand a knowledge base
- determining and establishing the conditions that help one become an effective learner (e.g., when, where, how to study)
- planning how and when to use cognitive strategies and applying them appropriately to a learning task
- actively connecting new information to information previously learned
- evaluating one's own success in a completed learning task
- recognizing the need for and seeking assistance appropriately from others (e.g., teachers, peers, specialists, community members)
- imitating the behaviors of native English speakers to complete tasks successfully
- knowing when to use native language resources (human and material) to promote understanding

Sample Progress Indicators

- scan several resources to determine the appropriateness to the topic of study
- skim chapter headings and bold print to determine the key points of a text
- take notes to summarize the main points provided in source material
- verbalize relationships between new information and information previously learned in another setting
- use verbal and nonverbal cues to know when to pay attention
- make pictures to check comprehension of a story or process
- scan an entry in a book to locate information for an assignment
- select materials from school resource collections to complete a project
- rehearse and visualize information
- take risks with language
- rephrase, explain, revise, and expand oral or written information to check comprehension
- seek more knowledgeable others with whom to consult to advance understanding
- seek out print and nonprint resources in the native language when needed

Grades 4–8

4–8 Vignette

Grade Level:	Fifth grade in an ESL pull-out class
English Proficiency Level:	Intermediate
Language of Instruction:	English
Focus of Instruction:	Social studies
Location:	Suburban school district in the South

Background

The following vignette describes an ESL class of four fifth-grade students, three girls and a boy, in a suburban elementary school. The teacher, Ms. Wilder, is monolingual and certified in ESL. She is conducting a 40-minute ESL class in a pull-out program. The students are Japanese children who are literate in their native language. They have low intermediate to intermediate proficiency levels in English. Because the students will be studying Native American Indians next week in their fifth-grade classroom, Ms. Wilder begins preparing them for that topic of study. In addition, she plans to cooperate with the fifth-grade teacher by modifying the regular classroom assignments to fit the needs and abilities of the ESOL children.

Instructional Sequence

During the two previous class sessions, Ms. Wilder taught skimming and scanning techniques to the four students. On this day, she assigns a different Native American tribe to student pairs and takes the students to the computer in the school library. She asks Yoriko to type in *Native American* and shows her how to press *subject* on the computer. Several book titles and call numbers appear for that subject, listing various tribes. At Ms. Wilder's suggestion, the students scan the list and Yoriko and her partner, Takeo, write the call numbers for books about their tribe. Takeo then suggests that they also look at the subjects, *Seminole Indians* or *Apaches,* because these are the two assigned tribes. Yoriko types the subject, *Seminoles,* into the computer. Several anthologies on Native American Indians that include Seminoles appear on the screen. Yoriko copies all relevant call numbers. She enters several of the call numbers and abstracts of the book appear. She and Takeo take notes as to what each book contains. The other student team repeats the process on the computer for the Apache tribe.

Ms. Wilder models how to use the call numbers to locate a book on the shelves. She gives the students a tour of the library and demonstrates how to find a book by looking in a specific section of the library, as indicted by the call number. The students watch attentively and then demonstrate their understanding as each student locates one of the resources identified from the computer. The students have call numbers for three different areas of the library. As they explore, they learn that reference books, such as encyclopedias, cannot be checked out, while nonfiction and fiction books can. Masago, a low intermediate-level student, checks with her peers in Japanese to be sure she understands this point correctly because she is unfamiliar with library procedures.

Ms. Wilder suggests that the students locate the books and reminds them to skim the table of contents for history, culture, religion, and modern day life. She asks Ryoko to review what they learned about skimming and scanning. The pairs look for books and skim the contents. They then scan the relevant chapters to see if the information they need is given and if they can understand the book. The students check out the books they have found so that they can continue this lesson during the next class. Yoriko and Takeo organize their books by subject on a shelf in their ESL classroom, so they can easily retrieve the books the next day. They plan to assist each other to select two books to bring to their fifth-grade classroom next week because each ESOL student belongs to separate groups in the regular classroom. After a week preparing their resources in the ESL class, the students will be able to share the books they find with the other fifth graders in their groups in the regular classroom.

Discussion

Students are encouraged to

▸ scan several resources to determine the appropriateness to the topic of study

▸ skim chapter headings and bold print to determine the key points of a text

▸ take notes to summarize the main points provided in source material

Ms. Wilder's ESL class is composed of four Japanese fifth graders. The students learn to use appropriate learning strategies that aid them in constructing and applying academic knowledge as required by their fifth-grade social studies curriculum. Ms. Wilder works with the regular classroom teacher to assist the ESOL students' understanding of the forthcoming unit, and to help them with specific tasks that they can complete ahead of time and share with their groups to facilitate academic learning.

By going to the library in a small group with their ESL teacher, the students are able to focus attention on the use of the computer and the organization of the library collection. They use technology as a resource to support their research efforts. By reading abstracts of catalogue entries on the library computer and taking notes, students are able to locate appropriate reference materials that they will use as part of a social studies project in their regular classroom. As needed, throughout the lesson, they check their comprehension in English and in the native language.

When Takeo suggests other ways to locate information from appropriate and varied sources, his idea assists the others in finding other pathways to gather information. The students work readily and successfully in pairs. They locate the books on the shelves following Ms. Wilder's modeling of this task and organize their materials for the next day's activities.

Yoriko, Takeo, Ryoko, and Masago are on their way to meeting the standard illustrated. They have focused on important aspects related to the completion of their assignment by actively seeking information. They have skimmed, scanned, and previewed material in English, after locating and gathering information from appropriate sources. Next week, when the lesson begins in their regular classroom, they will serve as resources to their groups, sharing the books they have selected as most appropriate. Each fifth-grade group will use, in part, the reference materials located by the ESOL students, thereby validating the ESOL students' learning experiences as contributing to the work of the group.

Grades 4–8

Goal 3, Standard 1

To use English in socially and culturally appropriate ways: Students will use the appropriate language variety, register, and genre according to audience, purpose, and setting

Descriptors

- using the appropriate degree of formality with different audiences and settings
- recognizing and using standard English and vernacular dialects appropriately
- using a variety of writing styles appropriate for different audiences, purposes, and settings
- responding to and using slang appropriately
- responding to and using idioms appropriately
- responding to and using humor appropriately
- determining when it is appropriate to use a language other than English
- determining appropriate topics for interaction

Sample Progress Indicators

- advise peers on appropriate language use
- prepare and deliver a short persuasive presentation to different audiences
- write a dialogue incorporating idioms or slang
- write business and personal letters
- create a commercial using an appropriate language style for the product
- create a cartoon or comic book
- initiate and carry on appropriate small talk (e.g., while visiting a classmate's home, on a bus, at a party)
- determine when it is appropriate to tell a joke
- use idiomatic speech appropriately
- advise peers on appropriate language use
- express humor through verbal and non-verbal means
- interact with an adult in a formal and informal setting
- role play a telephone conversation with an adult
- make polite requests
- use English and native languages appropriately in a multilingual social situation (e.g., cooperative games or team sports)
- write a letter or e-mail message to an adult or a peer using appropriate language forms
- demonstrate an understanding of ways to give and receive compliments, show gratitude, apologize, express anger or impatience
- greet and take leave appropriately in a variety of settings

4–8 Vignette

Grade Level: Seventh grade in a regular English class
English Proficiency Level: Low advanced
Language of Instruction: English
Focus of Instruction: Language arts
Location: Crow Indian Reservation in a Rocky Mountain state

Background

This vignette describes a seventh-grade English class on the Crow Indian Reservation in a Rocky Mountain state. All the students have low advanced proficiency in English, and all are Crow Indians. Most live in homes where Crow is the predominant language. Ms. Bender is a monolingual English-speaking teacher. During the first semester, she devotes each Friday's class period to teaching her students to identify and learn the meanings of idiomatic phrases the children are likely to encounter outside the reservation, and in which social contexts use of the idioms is appropriate or not appropriate.

Instructional Sequence

Every Thursday Ms. Bender hands out small notebooks to each student to take home for the night. For the next 24 hours, the students will be on an "idiom search," jotting in the notebooks any phrases they hear or see that they believe are idioms. Ms. Bender encourages them to find idioms using authentic sources, such as books, conversations, television programs, videos, movies, radio, music tapes, and CDs. During the first 10 minutes or so of Friday's class, the students write on the chalkboard the idioms they have found. Ms. Bender asks each student who writes an idiom on the board to try to define it according to the context in which it appeared. The other students offer their opinions about the phrases too. As needed, Ms. Bender then affirms or corrects the meanings. The students record new idioms in their notebooks.

Before the class began, Ms. Bender had written four idioms on construction paper and attached them to the wall. At this point, she divides the students into groups and reads each idiom. The first idiom is *fish out of water.* Ms. Bender uses the phrase in one or two sentences, such as "She was the only kid at the gathering, and so she felt like a fish out of water." Each group discusses the phrase's role in the sentence and then writes down a possible meaning. As a whole class, the groups share their definitions. This process continues for the next three idioms. At the end, Ms. Bender confirms or further explains the meanings and students also record these idioms and their meanings in the personal notebooks.

Ms. Bender then conducts a discussion on the social contexts in which the idioms raised in class that day can or should not be used. As an example, she says, "In the classroom, if one or two students are having difficulty with a task while the others are not, they should not be called *a fish out of water* because this would be considered impolite and rude." As a final activity, student groups prepare short dialogues that incorporate some of the new idioms in appropriate social contexts and read them aloud in front of the class.

Discussion

Students are encouraged to

▸ use idiomatic speech appropriately

▸ write a dialogue incorporating idioms or slang

All the students in Ms. Bender's class are Crow Indians and have low advanced proficiency in English. They are studying many idiomatic phrases that are common in mainstream society to develop the knowledge of when certain phrases are appropriate or not appropriate in different social contexts.

Ms. Bender has structured her lesson so that her students are actively involved in identifying idioms, learning in context, and determining correct usage of idiomatic expressions. She has the students "search" for idioms in their everyday environment. These searches lead to a class process where students work together to understand the meaning of idioms. The students discuss their idiom discoveries as well as the four idioms selected by the teacher in terms of their language usage, particularly the sociocultural settings in which a given idiom would be considered either appropriate or inappropriate. In their groups, they produce written definitions based on their discussion, then every student enters the new idioms and their meanings into a personal idiom notebook. Finally, they write dialogues to use the idioms in context and read their dialogues aloud in front of the class.

Because the use of language is a vital form of human behavior, the learning of idioms and their appropriate application demonstrates that Ms. Bender's students are achieving success in meeting this standard. She draws from the students' own encounters with idiomatic speech to facilitate this learning process.

Goal 3, Standard 2

To use English in socially and culturally appropriate ways: Students will use nonverbal communication appropriate to audience, purpose, and setting

Descriptors

- interpreting and responding appropriately to nonverbal cues and body language
- demonstrating knowledge of acceptable nonverbal classroom behaviors
- using acceptable tone, volume, stress, and intonation, in various social settings*
- recognizing and adjusting behavior in response to nonverbal cues

Sample Progress Indicators

- determine the appropriate distance to maintain while standing near someone, depending on the situation
- maintain appropriate level of eye contact with audience while giving an oral presentation
- demonstrate in a role play two aspects of body language common to one's own culture
- analyze nonverbal behavior
- describe intent by focusing on a person's nonverbal behavior
- add gestures to correspond to a dialogue in a play
- respond appropriately to a teacher's gesture
- obtain a teacher's attention in an appropriate manner
- use appropriate volume of voice in different settings such as the library, hall, gymnasium, supermarket, and movie theater

Grades 4–8

* For the purposes of this standard, TESOL considers tone, volume, stress, and intonation as part of nonverbal communication, along with physical manifestations of communication, such as gestures and proxemics.

4–8 Vignette

Grade Level:	Sixth grade in a regular class and an ESL pull-out class
English Proficiency Levels:	Mostly intermediate, some advanced
Language of Instruction:	English
Focus of Instruction:	Nonverbal communication styles
Location:	Suburban school district in the Midwest

Background

The following vignette describes Ms. Perlman's pull-out ESL classroom. The students come from Ms. Hess' sixth-grade classroom of 21 students, one third of whom are ESOL students. The ESOL students come from the Middle East, Central America, and India. Five of them are at an intermediate level of English proficiency, while the other two are advanced. The intermediate-level students are pulled out of their classroom to spend about an hour each day with Ms. Perlman, a certified ESL teacher. Ms. Hess and Ms. Perlman work very closely together; in fact, the preceding year, they were peer coaching partners.

Instructional Sequence

While the students are busy with an experiment on fossils, Ms. Hess notices some commotion in the group where Hanan is working and overhears comments by some of the Anglo students about Hanan being "in their face" all the time. This is the fourth time that an incident like this has occurred with Hanan as well as with two of the other ESOL students. Ms. Hess has observed that when the Arab and Latino girls are together, they stand very close to one another and touch each other frequently. She remembers thinking that she has also felt crowded by these girls when they were talking to her, and realized that some of these ESOL students stood closer to other people than she would. She talks to Ms. Perlman about this and they decide to try to make the girls aware of the different cultural norms of interaction related to the positioning of speakers' bodies during conversations. Ms. Perlman says she will focus on this issue some time in the near future in the daily ESL period that she has with those students.

Over the next couple of weeks, Ms. Perlman plans for this mini-lesson. She tapes segments from television programs and commercials that demonstrate interactions among people of varying ages. In class, she prepares the students for the discussion by slouching down in her chair and asking the students if they think it is appropriate for a teacher to sit that way in class and why. The students then make a list of inappropriate behaviors in and out of the classroom setting. Ms. Perlman moves the discussion to interaction styles and ends the session by showing the videotape and having students think about the rules that govern interactions in various contexts. For homework, the students are to take the list that they developed earlier and think about whether the same behaviors would be considered acceptable or unacceptable in their own cultures.

At the next session, the students discuss their findings and view the video segments again. Ms. Perlman narrows the discussion to focus the students' attention on acceptable distances that people maintain with one another as they interact. Leticia's suspicions about proximity norms in the U.S. culture are confirmed, whereas Hanan is perplexed by the different norms. Maha suggests to her that some Anglo students might be upset at times by the close distance that she and Hanan maintain.

Ms. Perlman is very satisfied and relieved with the way the discussion evolved, and when she reports back to Ms. Hess, they decide that they can talk about it openly with individual students as needed. Ms. Hess asks the ESOL students if they would present their findings to the full sixth-grade class.

Discussion

Students are encouraged to

- determine the appropriate distance to maintain while standing near someone, depending on the situation
- analyze nonverbal behavior

The ongoing, collaborative effort between Ms. Hess and Ms. Perlman clearly benefits the ESOL students. In this lesson, Ms. Hess, who is a good observer of behavior patterns, shares her concerns with Ms. Perlman. Ms. Perlman, through careful planning, prepares a lesson that allows the ESOL students to act as mini-ethnographers. Neither she nor Ms. Hess make a value judgment about cultural proximity norms. Rather, the students are asked to analyze nonverbal behavior on videotaped interactions drawn from television. At this stage, the students' own behaviors are not the focus.

The students begin by considering the appropriateness of certain behaviors according to the setting, such as in or out of school. Then through the videotape analysis activity, the ESOL students uncover some norms about proxemics. Within the ESL class, they are then able to discuss their own behaviors and place themselves in the shoes of some of their peers to determine what distances might be appropriate according to the people present. Ms. Hess validates the students' conclusions and has them present their findings to the class. The mainstream students and the teachers thereby benefit, learning about the different cultural proximity norms and perhaps adjusting their own behaviors and expectations accordingly.

Through the videotape analysis activity, the ESOL students uncover some norms about proxemics.

Grades 4–8

Goal 3, Standard 3

To use English in socially and culturally appropriate ways:
Students will use appropriate learning strategies to extend their
communicative competence

Descriptors

- observing and modeling how others speak and behave in a particular situation or setting
- experimenting with variations of language in social and academic settings
- seeking information about appropriate language use and behavior
- self-monitoring and self-evaluating language use according to setting and audience
- analyzing the social context to determine appropriate language use
- rehearsing variations of language use in different social and academic settings
- deciding when use of slang is appropriate

Sample Progress Indicators

- model behavior and language use of others in different situations and settings
- rephrase an utterance when it results in cultural misunderstanding
- evaluate behaviors in different situations
- observe language use and behaviors of peers in different settings
- rehearse different ways of speaking according to the formality of the setting
- test appropriate use of newly acquired gestures and language

Grades 4–8

4–8 Vignette

Grade Level:	Eighth grade in a bilingual class
English Proficiency Level:	Intermediate
Language of Instruction:	Khmer and English
Focus of Instruction:	Community service
Location:	Urban school district in the Northeast

Background

The following vignette describes Mr. Seng's eighth-grade class of 12 Cambodian students in their third year of a transitional bilingual education program. They are at an intermediate level of English proficiency and will make the transition out of the bilingual program next year when they enter high school. In their district, all middle school students are expected to perform 10 hours of community service. To accomplish that goal, Mr. Seng has arranged for the students to visit a nearby nursing home for 2 hours after school, one day a week for 5 weeks.

Instructional Sequence

Mr. Seng usually instructs his students in Khmer except for their English language arts course. At this point in the school year, March, however, he begins to include more English in all the subject areas to help prepare the students for their studies next year. He views the community service requirement of the social studies curriculum as an ideal means for helping his students practice English in a meaningful way. Beginning next Thursday, he and the class will walk to a local nursing home for a 2-hour visit in the afternoon. The patients at the nursing home are mostly Polish Americans and Greek Americans who have lived in the city for most of their lives.

Last week the director of the nursing home came to class and spoke to the students about the patients. She cautioned the students that some of the patients they will visit will be in wheelchairs or walkers. Others may have Alzheimer's disease or similar memory loss difficulties. She explained that they love to have visitors, and she intended to pair up each student with one patient. From time to time during her talk, Mr. Seng would interpret medical or other unfamiliar terminology in Khmer or ask one of the students to do so, thereby ensuring all the students understood the information.

This week Mr. Seng shows a clip from a television movie that has scenes in a nursing home. He asks the students to pay attention to the way the nurses and the family members speak to the patients. After viewing, they discuss as a class the way language was used. Students note that family members seemed to use *Grandma* or *Papa* or even *Dear,* while the nurses always used *Mr.* and *Mrs.* when addressing the patients. Mr. Seng asked the students how they might address their particular patient. All the students agree they would use titles, such as *Mr.* and *Mrs.* when they first meet. "Suppose one of the patients asks you to call her Sofia?" Mr. Seng asks. One student responds that he would not feel comfortable calling an elderly woman by her first name. "I would not do that in my culture. We try to show respect to the elderly," he explains in Khmer. Another student suggests that perhaps after they got to know each other, she might use a first name, if the patient insisted.

Next, Mr. Seng replays 4 minutes from the clip and asks students to write down one or two sentences from the dialogue. Upon request, he stops and replays an interchange so the students can write down all the words. Several students write their sentences on the board. The class comments on the choice of words and the type of grammar that was used by the characters in the scene. "The nurses seem to say 'Would you like something' every time." Mr. Seng concurs and explains that *Would you like* is a bit more formal. One student also comments that the patients, the nurses, and their visitors all spoke more slowly than most Americans that she encounters. "Why do you think that happens?" asks the teacher. Another student offers, "Maybe because they do not hear very well." Another student points out that everyone seemed to begin a conversation with a patient by asking how he or she was feeling.

Mr. Seng replays the full clip one last time and has the students take notes on the physical movements of the people who interacted with the patients. Afterwards, students discuss what happened, noting such things as who gave the patients hugs and kisses and who offered their hand, or how they helped the patients move around. One student remarked that the grandchild of one of the elderly patients repeatedly patted him on the head. "Is this something Americans do? In my country we do not touch the head."

As a final activity, Mr. Seng has the students role play several situations. Using the fish bowl technique, students sit on chairs that are placed in a circle. Three students take turns entering the circle to play a patient, nurse, and student visitor. Mr. Seng describes scenarios, such as: the first time the student and patient meet, a visit on the patient's birthday, a misunderstanding about patting one's head or arm on occasion, a visit when the patient must receive some medication, and the last visit scheduled for the class. Students practice what they will say and classmates give suggestions to improve the conversations.

Discussion

Students are encouraged to

- ‣ evaluate behaviors in different situations
- ‣ model behavior and language use of others in different situations and settings
- ‣ observe language use and behaviors of peers in different settings
- ‣ rehearse different ways of speaking according to the formality of the setting

Mr. Seng, in helping his students meet a school requirement and get ready for the mainstream classes they will attend the next year, designs a community service project that will place the students in an unfamiliar, sociocultural environment where they will need to be sensitive to their use of English and the cultural implications of their actions. He does not, however, immerse the students in the new environment without preparation. Before they are scheduled to visit the nursing home, he asks the director to talk with the class about what they should expect.

To further increase the students' awareness of language use and behavior and develop their skills in assessing appropriateness, Mr. Seng uses a television movie clip as a tool for data collection and reflection. By viewing the clip several times, the students can focus on the formality of the language use and the nonverbal gestures. They can make comparisons to their own cultural ways of behaving and addressing adults.

The role-play activity offers the students an opportunity to practice both what they have observed and have concluded about interacting with elderly patients in a nursing home. They rehearse different situations and interactions. They evaluate their classmates' role-play scenarios and make suggestions for adjusting language and behavior, as they deem appropriate. This practice opportunity also helps diminish the anxiety level the students might feel when they enter the English-only environment of the nursing home.

The role-play activity offers the students an opportunity to practice both what they have observed and have concluded about interacting with elderly patients in a nursing home.

Grades 4–8

Grades 9–12

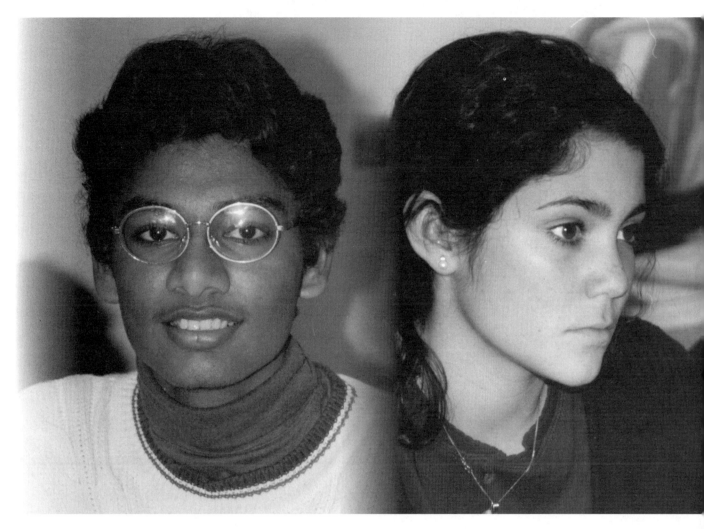

Syed Imran Haider and Catering Ramos in Alexandria, Virginia USA.

Goal 1, Standard 1

To use English to communicate in social settings:
Students will use English to participate in social interactions

Descriptors

- sharing and requesting information
- expressing needs, feelings, and ideas
- using nonverbal communication in social interactions
- getting personal needs met
- engaging in conversations
- conducting transactions

Sample Progress Indicators

- obtain, complete, and process application forms, such as driver's license, social security, college entrance
- express feelings through drama, poetry, or song
- make an appointment
- defend and argue a position
- use prepared notes in an interview or meeting
- ask peers for their opinions, preferences, and desires
- correspond with pen pals, English-speaking acquaintances, friends
- write personal essays
- make plans for social engagements
- shop in a supermarket
- engage listener's attention verbally or nonverbally
- volunteer information and respond to questions about self and family

- elicit information and ask clarification questions
- clarify and restate information as needed
- describe feelings and emotions after watching a movie
- indicate interests, opinions, or preferences related to class projects
- give and ask for permission
- offer and respond to greetings, compliments, invitations, introductions, and farewells
- negotiate solutions to problems, interpersonal misunderstandings, and disputes
- read and write invitations and thank you letters
- use the telephone

9–12 Vignette

Grade Level:	Twelfth grade in a self-contained ESL class
English Proficiency Level:	Advanced
Language of Instruction:	English
Focus of Instruction:	College application process
Location:	Urban school district in the East

Background

The following vignette describes a twelfth-grade, self-contained ESL transition class of advanced-level students in an Eastern urban school district. The class is composed of mostly Caribbean and Central American Spanish-speaking students. The students take a regular English literature class as well as this transitional ESL class. They are taught by Ms. Rodríguez, a bilingual Spanish/English-speaking teacher whose certification is in English. It is October of the senior year and the students are using English to navigate the college application process—from researching post-secondary institutions to practicing for an admissions interview.

Instructional Sequence

During this long-term project, which lasted for 4 weeks, students used various reference books and semantic mappings to identify their strengths, potential careers, and the kinds of colleges that would suit them. One of the students was reluctant to participate in these activities because he had no intention of going to college—as it was not in his family tradition, and he did not see a need for it. He discussed his feelings with two of his friends in class. Over the period of several days, they convinced him to join in the process, even if he did not plan to go to college. They explained to him that he might not want to go next year, but perhaps in the future he would. Also, they suggested the process would help for job applications and interviews.

After Ms. Rodríguez reviewed the elements of a business letter with the class, students wrote for college applications and catalogues. Once the application packets were received, the students worked in small groups to draft their essays. As a brainstorming activity before drafting the essay, the groups shared their career goals, hobbies, and interests, and the background characteristics that they felt a college might desire in its applicants. As a homework assignment, each student was to ask a peer or another teacher to list some positive features about himself or herself. The students were to gather information about their work ethic, potential, achievements, and so forth. The next day, the teacher presented several essays to the class and suggested the students consider one as a model for their own. The students then began working individually on their essays.

The next activity for the class focused on the admissions interview. The teacher showed the students a video with two sample interviews and pairs of students prepared lists of questions and personal notes to use in mock interviews. Some of these included: "Tell me about yourself." "What would you like to do after college?" "At this point in your life, what types of courses do

Grades 9–12

you want to explore?" and "What do you think about distance learning and video conferencing in place of sitting in a classroom with a professor?" The pairs exchange questions and conduct interviews, taking turns as the interviewer and interviewee.

Discussion

Students are encouraged to

- indicate interests, opinions, or preferences related to class projects
- write personal essays
- obtain, complete, and process application forms, such as driver's license, social security, college entrance
- use prepared notes in an interview or meeting
- ask peers for their opinions, preferences, and desires

The college application process is often confusing to high school seniors, native and nonnative speakers alike. Some immigrant students need more guidance and support because their families are less knowledgeable about the process. Some ESOL students, even those at advanced levels of proficiency, do not view themselves as "college material." One way to demystify the process is to break it down into discrete tasks as Ms. Rodríguez has done.

During this project, Ms. Rodríguez encourages her students to practice and apply many of the language activities they have learned over the years in a natural context with real tasks. Several of the planned activities have direct application to social situations in the real world. Students will write business letters, and they will go on interviews, whether for a college or for a job.

The students take responsibility for most of the work and interact with classmates to accomplish the tasks. They share information orally and in written form; they express ideas and give opinions; they write personal essays about themselves. They also ask others for opinions to gather information they can add to their application essays. When one student is uncomfortable with the project, the teacher allows him to discuss the situation and resolve it with his peers. In conducting mock interviews, the students learn the value of being prepared, such as anticipating the questions and taking notes in advance for possible responses.

> In conducting mock interviews, the students learn the value of being prepared, such as anticipating the questions and taking notes in advance for possible responses.

Grades 9–12

Goal 1, Standard 2

To use English to communicate in social settings:
Students will interact in, through, and with spoken and written
English for personal expression and enjoyment

Descriptors

- describing, reading about, or participating in a favorite activity
- sharing social and cultural traditions and values
- expressing personal needs, feelings, and ideas
- participating in popular culture

Sample Progress Indicators

- discuss preferences for types of music, book genres, and computer programs
- recommend a film or videotape to a friend
- write in a diary or personal journal
- describe, read, or write about a personal hero
- persuade peers to join in a favorite activity, game, or hobby
- discuss issues of personal importance or value
- locate information for leisure activities (in oral or written form)
- write a poem, short story, play, or song
- describe favorite storybook characters
- recommend a game, book, or computer program
- listen to, read, watch, and respond to plays, films, stories, books, songs, poems, computer programs, and magazines
- recount events of interest
- ask information questions for personal reasons
- make requests for personal reasons
- express enjoyment while playing a game
- talk about a favorite food or celebration
- express humor through verbal and non-verbal means

Grades 9–12

9–12 Vignette

Grade Level:	Tenth grade in a transitional ESL/language arts class
English Proficiency Level:	Advanced
Language of Instruction:	English
Focus of Instruction:	Language arts
Location:	Urban school district in the Southwest

Background

The following vignette describes a transitional language arts class that prepares ESOL students for a mainstream class the following year. It is taught by a certified English teacher with a masters degree in ESL. Most of the students are native Spanish speakers; a few speak Hindi or Japanese. Instruction is offered in English, but the teacher, Mr. Collins, uses Spanish and the students use their native languages on occasion, primarily for clarification. The advanced ESOL students will receive one full English credit for this class when they complete it in June. The high school is located in a city in Arizona.

Instructional Sequence

Every spring *The Arizona Chronicle* sponsors a poetry contest for high school students. Mr. Collins shared the newspaper's announcement with his class. Several students indicated their interest in the competition. Viewing it as a voluntary activity, Mr. Collins arranged to meet with interested students at the end of the school day to form an after-school poetry club. Although as a class they had read and analyzed poems, Mr. Collins had never assigned poem composition as a required task. Therefore at this first meeting after school, the students and Mr. Collins spent most of the time discussing strategies for writing poems. Mr. Collins explained that many poets write poems about personal experiences or joys or concerns. Aya, a Japanese student, remarked that she occasionally wrote haiku and drew her inspiration from nature. She agreed to share two of her poems about the desert with the group the following day. In the meantime, Mr. Collins encouraged the students to keep journals, recording encounters, sights, commonplace or unusual happenings, along with their feelings at the time. These journals would be a source for poems.

The students followed Mr. Collins' advice and several began to read poetry books on their own as well. On occasion the group met after school and debated the value of rhyme and meter, works of Pablo Neruda and Maya Angelou, distinctions between metaphor and description, and use of adverbs and adjectives. They began to write some poems to read to one another and solicit feedback. Mr. Collins was careful to act as a member of the group, not as a teacher, nor as the sole advisor. He too wrote some poems to share, and although he occasionally provided technical information, the students ran the poetry group for the most part by themselves. After 6 weeks, each member had a poem ready to submit to the newspaper's contest. Even after the submissions had been sent, the group continued to meet for the rest of the school year.

Discussion

Students are encouraged to

- write a poem, short story, play, or song
- write in a diary or personal journal
- listen to, read, watch, and respond to plays, films, stories, books, songs, poems, computer programs, and magazines

The poetry group was formed because of the students' personal interest in writing poetry. The English teacher acted as a catalyst in pointing out the newspaper's annual contest to the students and providing some technical advice. These ESOL students, all at an advanced level, accepted the challenge, began to read poetry during their free time, kept a journal as many writers do, and wrote and shared poems. The teacher was a colleague in the process, a member of the group. The students used English to read poems and write their own, to discuss poems read and written, and to debate techniques of poem construction. Their enjoyment of the activity became evident when they decided to continue the poetry group even after their poems had been submitted to the newspaper.

Grades 9–12

Goal 1, Standard 3

To use English to communicate in social settings:
Students will use learning strategies to extend their
communicative competence

Descriptors

- testing hypotheses about language
- listening to and imitating how others use English
- exploring alternative ways of saying things
- focusing attention selectively
- seeking support and feedback from others
- comparing nonverbal and verbal cues
- self-monitoring and self-evaluating language development
- using the primary language to ask for clarification
- learning and using language "chunks"
- selecting different media to help understand language
- practicing new language
- using context to get meaning

Sample Progress Indicators

- make notes in preparation for a meeting or interview
- plan and rehearse an anticipated conversation
- use a dictionary to validate choice of language
- ask a classmate whether a particular word or phrase is correct
- use a computer spell checker to verify spelling
- use written sources to discover or check information
- keep individual notes for language learning
- test appropriate use of new vocabulary, phrases, and structures
- ask someone the meaning of a word
- understand verbal directions by comparing them with nonverbal cues (e.g., folding paper into eighths, lining up)
- tell someone in the native language that a direction given in English was not understood
- recite poems or songs aloud or to oneself
- imitate a classmate's response to a teacher's question or directions
- associate realia or diagrams with written labels to learn vocabulary or construct meaning
- practice recently learned language by teaching a peer

9–12 Vignette

Grade Level: Eleventh grade in a sheltered content class
English Proficiency Level: Intermediate
Language of Instruction: English
Focus of Instruction: Driver's education
Location: Suburban school district in the West

Background

This vignette describes an intermediate-level, sheltered content class with students from a variety of language backgrounds in a suburban setting. The class is studying driver's education, and the students have not yet driven. The teacher, Mr. Murphy, has an ESL endorsement. For this class session, he invited Officer Louis to talk about the dangers of driving.

Instructional Sequence

Officer Louis plans to show a short video of teenage car accidents. He introduces the video with a lecture about different causes of car accidents, such as poor car maintenance, excess speed, and peer pressure to drive recklessly, and asks the students to look for the cause of each accident shown in the video. As Officer Louis speaks, Mr. Murphy writes key words on the board for later reference. Before the video begins, Mai Lin, who has a hearing impairment, moves her seat nearer the VCR monitor. She adjusts her amplification device once the sound begins.

Huynh did not fully understand the officer's lecture. He heard the words *excess speed*. He knows speed means "fast," but he did not understand what excess speed might mean. While watching the video, he notices the camera zooms onto a speed limit sign that says 65 and then zooms onto the car's speedometer, which shows 80. He thinks, "Perhaps excess means too much." He turns to Thuy and asks him in Vietnamese whether excess means "too much." Thuy confirms that it does.

After students have viewed the video, Mr. Murphy and Officer Louis review the video and key terms. Mr. Murphy asks, "Does anyone know what *excess speed* means?" Huynh volunteers, "I think it means *too much*." "How did you figure that out?" the police officer asks. "80 is more than 65," replies Huynh. Mr. Murphy praises his strategy, "That's good, Huynh. You used the video pictures to understand the term."

Next, Officer Louis puts students in pairs with the state's driving code manual. He asks the students to determine which rules were broken and what caused each of the accidents shown in the video.

Mai Lin and Christina work together. They sit side by side so Christina can speak directly into Mai Lin's hearing aid. Christina suggests one rule that was broken. "In the second accident, the driver turned in the wrong place." Mai Lin questions Mr. Murphy about ways to check their answers. He reminds her of the diagrams and recommends she refer to the code manual.

Christina remembers that there was a sign on the road just before the accident happened. She searches through the book and matches the sign she remembers with the no-U-turn sign and reads the rule to Mai Lin. Mai Lin agrees, "Oh. That's the rule the driver broke. No U-turn."

Discussion

Students are encouraged to

- ask a classmate whether a particular word or phrase is correct
- use written sources to discover or check information
- associate realia or diagrams with written labels to learn vocabulary or construct meaning

In this vignette, Huynh hypothesizes the meaning of *excess* by relating Officer Louis's spoken language with the visuals he saw in the video. This strategy allows him to understand language he has not encountered before and to learn its meaning. He then checks his hypothesis with his peer, Thuy, in Vietnamese. This strategy allows him to validate his hypothesis. Mr. Murphy also helps his class by recording key terms on the board as the police officer speaks and then reviewing them after the students have seen the video. This strategy particularly benefits Mai Lin who needs some occasional accommodations in class to compensate for her hearing loss.

As Mai Lin and Christina work to determine the causes of the accidents, they ask Mr. Murphy for some assistance. He reminds them to recall the video and examine the diagrams in the driving code manual. Because Mai Lin agrees with Christina's suggestions that the car turned in the wrong place, they check in the book for the visual Christina remembered seeing to find the correct term for it. By using this strategy, they learn the expression, *U-turn,* and find the related driving rule.

Mr. Murphy also helps his class by recording key terms on the board as the police officer speaks and then reviewing them after the students have seen the video.

Grades 9–12

Goal 2, Standard 1

To use English to achieve academically in all content areas:
Students will use English to interact in the classroom

Descriptors

- following oral and written directions, implicit and explicit
- requesting and providing clarification
- participating in full-class, group, and pair discussions
- asking and answering questions
- requesting information and assistance
- negotiating and managing interaction to accomplish tasks
- explaining actions
- elaborating and extending other people's ideas and words
- expressing likes, dislikes, and needs

Sample Progress Indicators

- interpret a teacher's indirect command to behave appropriately
- ask a teacher or peer to confirm one's understanding of directions to complete an assignment
- justify changes in assignments or the need for an extension
- request supplies to complete an assignment
- use polite forms to negotiate and reach consensus
- follow directions to form groups
- negotiate cooperative roles and task assignments
- take turns when speaking in a group
- modify a statement made by a peer
- paraphrase a teacher's directions orally or in writing
- respond to a teacher's general school-related small talk
- explain the reason for being absent or late to a teacher
- negotiate verbally to identify role in preparation for a group/class presentation
- ask a teacher to restate or simplify directions
- join in a group response at the appropriate time
- listen to and incorporate a peer's feedback regarding classroom behavior
- greet a teacher when entering class
- distribute and collect classroom materials
- share classroom materials and work successfully with a partner
- ask for assistance with a task

9–12 Vignette

Grade Level:	Tenth grade in a self-contained ESL class
English Proficiency Level:	Low intermediate
Language of Instruction:	English
Focus of Instruction:	Language arts
Location:	Suburban school district in the Southwest

Background

The following vignette describes a tenth-grade ESL class in a Southwest suburban high school. All of the 21 students are native Spanish speakers who have been in the United States from 1 to 2 years. Most of the students arrived from Mexico and were literate in Spanish. However, three of the students had limited formal schooling before coming to the United States. On the whole, the class is at a low intermediate-level of English proficiency. Several students are more comfortable writing and reading than they are speaking. The students in this class have two periods of ESL instruction daily. Their teacher is an experienced, certified English speaker who recently has completed her masters degree in ESL education. She speaks Spanish and uses it on occasion in the class.

Instructional Sequence

As the ESOL students enter the classroom, Ms. Judson greets each of them and asks how they are. She uses a variety of phrases: "Good morning." " Hi. How are you?" "How's it going?" "How are you feeling?" She also asks individual students some questions about other classes, assignments, tests, presentations, and so forth. Ms. Judson generally spends the first few minutes of class in this way; she calls this a warm-up. Two of the students have been absent for a couple of days and Ms. Judson asks them why. José replies, "I was sick." Rafael nods his head and says, "Me too. I had a flu. I couldn't finish my reading paper. Could I stay after school? I have some questions for you." Ms. Judson agrees to meet with him later.

For the past few weeks, Ms. Judson has been working with this class on literature response. In her regular English classes, she engages the students in reading and responding to poems, short stories, and novels, and she wants her ESOL students to have the same kind of experiences. Two weeks earlier she had explained to the students that the focus of the literature study is their own personal response to literature—what they think and feel about what they are reading.

Since that time, Ms. Judson has worked to engage all of the students in sharing their ideas and feelings. More students are responding now, but she is dissatisfied with how the students listen and converse with each other. Virtually all of the comments are directed to her, and the students do not listen to and respond to each others' comments. She decides to try to demonstrate how she wants the students to work together. She asks the students to sit in two circles with the classroom chairs making an inner circle and an outer circle.

She distributes copies of a Piri Thomas poem, " La Peseta," about a teenage boy caught taking money from his father's dresser. The poem is lighthearted, and some Spanish is sprinkled throughout. Ms. Judson tells the students that she is going to read the poem and then ask the inner circle of students to talk about their reactions. She tells the students that she is not going to respond this time; she is going to take notes on what they say. She also asks the students in the outer circle to pay close attention to what the ones in the inner circle are doing. "How do they behave with each other? How do they work together?"

Ms. Judson reads the poem out loud and then says, "So, what do you want to say about this poem? How do you respond?" She then lowers her head and prepares to write. Some students in the outer circle begin to chat quietly. Ms Judson looks up and clears her throat. Jasmine elbows Rosa, and they settle down. After some silence and shuffling, one student in the inner circle comments and then another. Because Ms. Judson does not make eye contact with the group members, they gradually begin to make eye contact with each other and pay more attention to what each person is saying. They begin to build on previous statements, agreeing or disagreeing, as they become more conversational.

After about 10 minutes, Ms. Judson stops the discussion and asks the students in the outer circle to comment on what they saw. The first few remarks focus on the content of what the inner circle group said. Ms. Judson acknowledges these observations but explains that she wants the students to think about how the students treated each other. "How did they behave? What did they do in the group?" Eventually, one of the students offers, "They looked at each other." Another says, "They listen, they pay attention. One student says what she thinks." Ms. Judson writes down the students' comments.

Finally, Ms. Judson summarizes what she heard the students say about how the group worked together and adds her own comments about the discussion. "We heard you use English in a number of different ways. For instance, you used English to agree and disagree, saying things like, 'I don't think he should have asked his father first' or 'I agree he needs to learn to act better.' You also asked questions if you didn't understand what someone meant or you rephrased your remark so the others could understand. Most of you also gave reasons for your opinions." She suggests that the students think about the interaction, because this might be helpful for them in future group work.

In the days that follow, Ms. Judson continues to work with literature response, using some poems by Gary Soto and short stories by Piri Thomas and Sandra Cisneros. She notices that more of the students are listening to each other and attending to others' comments instead of paying attention only to her and her comments.

Discussion

Students are encouraged to

- respond to a teacher's general school-related small talk
- explain the reason for being absent or late to a teacher
- listen to and incorporate a peer's feedback regarding classroom behavior
- interpret a teacher's indirect command to behave appropriately
- justify changes in assignments or the need for an extension

Ms. Judson believes that one of the functions of the ESL classroom is to prepare students for mainstream classes by providing some of the same experiences they will have there. Therefore, she incorporates activities such as literature response in her lessons. She likes this activity because it gives her students multiple opportunities to speak English, when some are reluctant to do so.

Each class period begins with small talk. Ms. Judson wants the students to be comfortable with the type of casual interaction that takes place between teachers and students. José and Rafael are able to explain an absence as well as a reason for not completing an assignment. Rafael asks for the teacher's assistance in finishing the task.

For literature study, Ms. Judson chooses poems and short stories by Hispanic authors. She believes that her ESOL students will relate well to these selections culturally and personally. She reads the texts out loud while the students follow along, as a strategy to assist students with limited formal schooling.

Ms. Judson has found that it is most effective to demonstrate the classroom behaviors she wants the students to engage in and then talk about them. Therefore, she asks some of the students to watch the others as they respond to the poem and then analyze what they did. To keep the students on task, Ms. Judson uses some indirect commands, such as throat clearing and eyebrow raising. Her students have learned to interpret these appropriately and modify their behavior. Jasmine used a nonverbal gesture to communicate with Rosa.

Because many of the ESOL students are less used to speaking up and being "on stage," the inner and outer circle technique worked well. Students inside needed to listen and respond to peer's comments, and feedback from the outer circle peers on the inner circle interaction was useful in later lessons with literature response components. The students demonstrated their ability to use English for a variety of conversational functions, such as agreement, justification, and clarification. Ms. Judson hopes that with the in-class emphasis on listening and conversing, her ESOL students will eventually feel comfortable conversing with non-ESOL students.

> Ms. Judson has found that it is most effective to demonstrate the classroom behaviors she wants the students to engage in and then talk about them.

9–12 Vignette

Grade Level: Eleventh–twelfth grade in a dental careers class

English Proficiency Level: Intermediate to advanced

Language of Instruction: English

Focus of Instruction: Computer technology

Location: Suburban school district in the Northwest

Background

The following vignette describes an introductory dental careers class located in a professional technical center in a large suburban school district. Students learn theoretical foundations of dentistry and perform basic technical skills in a simulated laboratory setting. The teacher, Mrs. Mason, is a monolingual English speaker with minimal training in working with ESOL students. The class is composed of eleventh- and twelfth-grade students of whom approximately 50% are ESOL students with intermediate to nearly nativelike proficiency in English. ESOL students come from South America, Korea, Vietnam, the Ukraine, and the Middle East.

Instructional Sequence

In today's lesson, Mrs. Mason has taken students to the Internet lab to locate articles or information related to dental careers, which they will then summarize in their article summary journals. This is the first time the entire class has visited the lab. Some students have virtually no experience with Internet research, while others have enough experience that they are able to assist classmates with problems. Mrs. Mason offers the students the option of working with a partner at the computer, although each student must select a separate article.

Entering the lab, each student signs in at a terminal and follows Mrs. Mason's instructions to start the Internet browser software and select a search engine. They then begin their searches by entering key words. Ana and Shannon, who are partners, have some trouble following the instructions and ask Bryce for assistance. Bryce explains how to get to the search screen, where to enter the key word, and so forth. Some other students are undecided as to which topic they want to investigate first. Mrs. Mason invites the class to brainstorm a few possible key words and phrases, which she then writes on the white board: *dentist* or *dentistry, orthodontia* or *orthodontics, periodontal disease, oral cancer, tooth decay.* The lab buzzes with conversation as students confer on selection and spelling of key words, and, when their search results are unsatisfactory, ask and offer advice on finding alternatives that may produce the desired information.

Students review their results in order to select a suitable article, sometimes taking brief notes. Monica scans the list of document summaries and identifies those that best match her search parameters. Huma, however, finds it difficult to decide from the summaries which articles are most appropriate for the assignment and asks Mrs. Mason for some guidance. Mrs. Mason helps her determine which of the documents are advertisements for dental office services, which are general information, and which are highly technical journal articles. Huma then chooses several articles that appear to be best suited to her reading level and knowledge of the subject, and skims them quickly before making her selection.

A minor technical problem complicates the class's attempts to print their selected articles: The printer only accepts print commands from two computer stations. While Mrs. Mason and a few experienced students check the other terminals, most of the students copy the World Wide Web addresses of their chosen documents and then negotiate with JT and Freddy to use their terminals to issue print commands. Several students cluster around the printer, identifying and distributing articles as they are printed. Groups of students informally compare articles and, in several instances, make exchanges. Marcelo, who dislikes reading from a computer screen, is dissatisfied with his article once he reads the hard copy and compares it to Tania's article. Then he quickly returns to his station and uses Tania's advice to find a more appropriate article containing illustrations and charts that help him understand the technical content. By the end of the lab session, all the students have selected and printed an article to summarize in their journals.

Discussion

Students are encouraged to

- ask a teacher or peer to confirm their understanding of directions to complete an assignment
- negotiate cooperative roles and task assignments
- ask for assistance with a task
- share classroom materials and work successfully with a partner

Mrs. Mason's class is a diverse group of juniors and seniors, of whom approximately half are nonnative speakers of English, with skills ranging from intermediate to nearly nativelike proficiency. Mrs. Mason has structured the activity so that students conduct academic research with classmates in the computer lab environment, using and developing both English language skills and Internet research skills in an authentic context.

As they work on the assignment, some students need assistance and use English to request help. Ana and Shannon turn to Bryce when they cannot follow the teacher's directions about starting their search on the Internet. Huma asks Mrs. Mason for help in identifying appropriate articles. Other students advise one another on key word search strategies and later compare articles, resulting in some exchanges. Once Marcelo expresses dissatisfaction with the first article he printed, Tania helps him find an article that is more suitable for his reading level. The students also work together when a technical problem arises with the printer. Using their English skills, they negotiate printing options and share the computer equipment that is connected to the printer.

Goal 2, Standard 2

To use English to achieve academically in all content areas: Students will use English to obtain, process, construct, and provide subject matter information in spoken and written form

Descriptors

- comparing and contrasting information
- persuading, arguing, negotiating, evaluating, and justifying
- listening to, speaking, reading, and writing about subject matter information
- gathering information orally and in writing
- retelling information
- selecting, connecting, and explaining information
- analyzing, synthesizing, and inferring from information
- responding to the work of peers and others
- representing information visually and interpreting information presented visually
- hypothesizing and predicting
- formulating and asking questions
- understanding and producing technical vocabulary and text features according to content area
- demonstrating knowledge through application in a variety of contexts

Sample Progress Indicators

- compare and classify information using technical vocabulary
- prepare for and participate in a debate
- take notes as a teacher presents information or during a film in order to summarize key concepts
- synthesize, analyze, and evaluate information
- write a summary of a book, article, movie, or lecture
- locate information appropriate to an assignment in text or reference materials
- research information on academic topics from multiple sources
- take a position and support it orally or in writing
- construct a chart synthesizing information
- identify and associate written symbols with words (e.g., written numerals with spoken numbers, the compass rose with directional words)
- define, compare, and classify objects (e.g., according to number, shape, color, size, function, physical characteristics)
- explain change (e.g., growth in plants and animals, in seasons, in self, in characters in literature)
- record observations
- construct a chart or other graphic showing data
- read a story and represent the sequence of events (through pictures, words, music, or drama)
- locate reference material
- generate and ask questions of outside experts (e.g., about their jobs, experiences, interests, qualifications)
- gather and organize the appropriate materials needed to complete a task
- edit and revise own written assignments
- use contextual clues
- consult print and nonprint resources in the native language when needed

9–12 Vignette

Grade Level:	Eleventh grade in a mainstream civics class
English Proficiency Level:	Advanced
Language of Instruction:	English
Focus of Instruction:	Civics
Location:	Urban school district in the Northeast

Background

The following vignette describes an eleventh-grade, one-semester civics course, which is composed of 24 advanced ESOL students and mainstream English-speaking students, in a Northeast urban high school. The majority of the students are of Hispanic background. Most ESOL students speak Spanish; other language groups include Haitian and Chinese. Mr. Philippe, the teacher, is certified in both civics and English as a second language. He is proficient in Haitian Creole and English, and has a working knowledge of Spanish. Most of the students in this class are true advanced-level students, although some are more at the intermediate level. The students' ages range from 16 to 19. It is near the end of the school year.

Instructional Sequence

Recognizing the importance of the development of academic skills at the advanced level, Mr. Philippe has developed a series of lesson activities that will take approximately 1 full week to cover in a class that meets for 80 minutes every day. The lesson activities are centered around the theme of civic responsibility and include discussions of what it means to be an informed citizen and how one takes action regarding a community concern. The week-long project requires small student groups to research information from multiple sources and prepare for a debate to compare and contrast points of view on a topic generated by the class during the first day: a toxic waste dump planned for their neighborhood. Six groups of four students are formed and they are given the task of comparing and contrasting articles from different newspapers, magazines, public interest groups' literature, and on-line sources. Whenever necessary, students of the same language discuss difficult ideas in their native language. Some teammates who are native speakers of English explain vocabulary and cultural dimensions to the assignment, such as the value of picketing. The students have had prior experiences comparing and contrasting reading selections and doing some library-based research.

As the research continues throughout the week, Mr. Philippe occasionally calls the class together to share their findings. The ideas and issues that begin to crystallize are recorded on newsprint and mounted on the walls for further discussion. Positions and resolutions are compared and contrasted at times, using graphic organizers. Whenever necessary, the teacher asks open-ended questions based on the resources in order to guide students' reactions and understandings of the articles' ideas, photographs, graphics (e.g., charts), language, and tone. In some instances, they discuss bias-related elements in the research materials.

On the fourth day, students begin practicing for the debate. At this point, Mr. Philippe assigns the positions. Three teams join to represent the side in favor of the dump; the three other teams will oppose it. From the 12 students on each side, peers select 3 to present the case at Friday's debate. The others help plan the points to be offered and critique the practice performances.

After the debate is held, students are asked to write individual essays in which they describe which debate team was more convincing and why. They are then asked to take a position on the debate and support it in writing based upon their own informed perspectives.

Discussion

Students are encouraged to

- locate information appropriate to an assignment in text or reference materials
- research information on academic topics from multiple sources
- take a position and support it orally or in writing
- compare and classify information using technical vocabulary
- prepare for and participate in a debate

Mr. Philippe recognizes the importance of a classroom environment that is conducive to language acquisition and learning. One way learning occurs is through meaningful activities, so he allows his students to select the topic they will explore for the civics assignment. He also provides his students with direction and material in order to build on their prior background and experiences. Through sharing and discussing, analyzing language and organizing information, responding to text, and working in groups and as a whole class, the students participate in activities that develop their academic English, integrating all four language strands.

Students research information and generate opinions about a topic of interest to their lives within the context of the civics curriculum. They locate multiple sources of information and through class discussion come to understand the different genres in which information can be shared as well as the potential biases that writers can include in their material. This helps the students develop an awareness of the power and impact of language.

Students in Mr. Philippe's class also acknowledge one another as resources and look to classmates for assistance. For example, native-English-speaking students and those who are not recent immigrants are able to act as cultural informants with respect to civic action. Mr. Philippe, likewise, allows more proficient students to explain concepts in the native language of their peers.

The students are also called upon to use their cognitive abilities as they prepare for a debate. They must clarify their own positions, argue persuasively, and anticipate the arguments of their opponents. In a supportive environment, students rehearse with their teammates' guidance. Help in this regard is further provided by the teacher's planned activities for comparing and contrasting viewpoints with the class as a whole. The recorded ideas, issues, and observations remain on the newsprint in sight of the students throughout the week.

Through sharing and discussing, analyzing language and organizing information, responding to text, and working in groups and as a whole class, the students participate in activities that develop their academic English, integrating all four language strands.

Grades 9–12

After the group activity is completed, Mr. Philippe gives a writing assignment that permits him to assess the knowledge individual students have acquired. The students argue a position in an essay drawing from the syntheses and analyses of information that they made in their groups and from their responses to the debate they observed.

9–12 Vignette

Grade Level:	16- to 21-year-olds in an alternative high school
English Proficiency Level:	Beginning to intermediate
Language of Instruction:	English
Focus of Instruction:	Vocational education
Location:	Suburban school district in a Rocky Mountain State

Background

Mr. Sánchez is a bilingual teacher who acts as a resource to the vocational education program at an alternative high school in a Rocky Mountain State. Older students, aged 16-21, attend this school. Spanish-speaking students have core curriculum courses in Spanish for half the day and vocational courses in English the other half. In the following vignette, Mr. Sánchez works with the Spanish-speaking students from Mr. Feehan's vocational class, using sheltered instruction techniques to teach about safety in English.

Instructional Sequence

Mr. Feehan's Building Trades class has been studying safety, and he has requested help for some students who are having difficulty understanding the vocabulary involved. Dressed in carpenter's overalls, Mr. Sánchez greets the students as they enter the room. Mr. Sánchez has safety goggles around his neck, a tool belt with various tools on it, and workboots with steel toes. Mr. Sánchez refers to the safety guidebook that they have been studying and asks them what their understanding of safety is. "What is safety? Why do we study about it?" There are several answers about saving lives, and one student mentions preventing accidents. The teacher encourages this student to give an example of how safety might prevent an accident, and he talks about clothing, which, conveniently, is the first topic to be covered today.

At this point, Mr. Sánchez asks the class how many of them work in the construction field. Several of them raise their hands. The teacher asks them what they think the most important points about dressing safely are and why, based on their own experience. A good discussion follows, so a list of the most important points to remember is generated on an overhead transparency. Mr. Sánchez then uses an overhead projector with diagrams and pictures to illustrate what appropriate dress for a building trades professional should be.

The students are asked to form pairs, read the corresponding pages in their safety guidebooks, underline the most important words and phrases, and help each other clarify meaning. Afterwards, a student records the underlined terms on the board and then the class compares them with the list generated earlier. Finally, Mr. Sánchez asks if there are any words which they still do not understand and explains them through demonstrations, pictures, or objects at hand.

Showing a picture of a sloppily dressed worker on a transparency, Mr. Sánchez asks the students to identify what is wrong with him. They note the baggy pants that are worn too low and therefore a possible hazard in terms of tripping. He has sandals on instead of workboots. He is wearing jewelry: rings that could crush a finger and chains that could catch on moving machinery. His shirt is too loose as well and might catch in a moving saw blade. They also notice that he does not have safety glasses visible anywhere.

Another picture is shown of the same worker all cleaned up with his shirt tucked in, his pants pulled up and buckled, workboots clean, and a hardhat in place. One of the students points out that this individual had long hair in the first picture and asks what had happened to that. A good demonstration of how to tie up long hair under a hardhat is offered by an experienced class member. Another brief discussion follows about hair and jewelry and getting and keeping a job. Mr. Sánchez displays the two pictures of the same worker, sloppy and neat, and asks the class whom they would hire if they had to choose. The answers are unanimously in favor of the neat worker.

The students engage in an open-ended discussion about how clothing is a safety issue as well as an employability issue sometimes. The class critiques Mr. Sánchez's overalls and general appearance, too. The class concludes with an assignment to reread the section on tool safety the next day.

Discussion

Students are encouraged to

▸ identify and associate written symbols with words (e.g., written numerals with spoken numbers, the compass rose with directional words)

▸ define, compare, and classify objects (e.g., according to number, shape, color, size, function, physical characteristics)

▸ use contextual clues

▸ generate and ask questions of outside experts (e.g., about their jobs, experiences, interests, qualifications)

Mr. Sánchez provided listening and speaking activities for the students in the bilingual program to enhance their reading comprehension on the topic of safety. He motivated them by "personalizing" the topic of safety. Several students described their own experiences doing construction work and the whole class discussed safety issues at the work site. Building on student knowledge, Mr. Sánchez used probing open-ended questions to help students focus on safety procedures in the workplace: "What is safety? Why do we study safety—to pass a test or to prevent an accident, injury or death?"

The students drew conclusions about proper workplace attire by analyzing Mr. Sánchez's clothing and critiquing the overhead transparency images. On one occasion, a student asked, "What are *workboots*?" Mr. Sánchez showed him his boots and explained how they were different and why they had a steel toe. The lesson material was presented by written word, pictures in the text, authentic materials, overhead transparencies, and modeled by the instructor. It was reinforced through discussion. By the end of class, the students recognized proper attire for construction settings.

Building on student knowledge, Mr. Sánchez used probing open-ended questions to help students focus on safety procedures in the workplace.

The students learned safety vocabulary pertaining to clothing in a variety of ways. They talked about it and listed important concepts and words on the board; they read about safety in their books and noted words to learn. Mr. Sánchez also used diagrams on an overhead projector and wore an appropriate work uniform so students could see the real items. Through these various presentations that addressed different learning styles, the students learned the vocabulary easily. The subsequent classes on tool safety were presented the same way and the results were equally as successful. The students later passed the required safety test, performing better than the students who had not been similarly instructed.

Goal 2, Standard 3

To use English to achieve academically in all content areas: Students will use appropriate learning strategies to construct and apply academic knowledge

Descriptors

- focusing attention selectively
- applying basic reading comprehension skills such as skimming, scanning, previewing, and reviewing text
- using context to construct meaning
- taking notes to record important information and aid one's own learning
- applying self-monitoring and self-corrective strategies to build and expand a knowledge base
- determining and establishing the conditions that help one become an effective learner (e.g., when, where, how to study)
- planning how and when to use cognitive strategies and applying them appropriately to a learning task
- actively connecting new information to information previously learned
- evaluating one's own success in a completed learning task
- recognizing the need for and seeking assistance appropriately from others (e.g., teachers, peers, specialists, community members)
- imitating the behaviors of native English speakers to complete tasks successfully
- knowing when to use native language resources (human and material) to promote understanding

Sample Progress Indicators

- preview assigned textbook chapters and generate questions to explore the topics to be presented

- establish the preconditions necessary for effective study (e.g., noise level, seating arrangements, access to needed materials)
- practice an oral report with a peer prior to presenting it in class
- evaluate a written assignment using rating criteria provided by the teacher
- brainstorm ideas with native language peers prior to writing a composition on a given topic
- scan several resources to determine the appropriateness to the topic of study
- skim chapter headings, and bold print to determine the key points of a text
- take notes to summarize the main points provided in source material
- verbalize relationships between new information and information previously learned in another setting
- use verbal and nonverbal cues to know when to pay attention
- make pictures to check comprehension of a story or process
- scan an entry in a book to locate information for an assignment
- select materials from school resource collections to complete a project
- rehearse and visualize information
- take risks with language
- rephrase, explain, revise, and expand oral or written information to check comprehension
- seek more knowledgeable others with whom to consult to advance understanding
- seek out print and nonprint resources in the native language when needed

9–12 Vignette

Grade Level: Ninth–eleventh in a nongraded, regular math class

English Proficiency Level: Beginning

Language of Instruction: English

Focus of Instruction: Consumer math

Location: Rural school district in the Southwest

Background

The following vignette describes a high school consumer math class in a rural school district. The teacher, Mr. Jones, is a monolingual English speaker with minimal training in working with ESOL students. The class is predominantly white, non-ESOL students spanning Grades 9–11. There are three ESOL students, all Hispanic and recently arrived from Mexico; one student has limited formal schooling.

Instructional Sequence

Mr. Jones' class has been studying a unit on measurement. To date, students have learned to measure and calculate surface area and volume in preparation for a hands-on construction project that they will undertake, namely, redecorating the classroom and building some bookshelves. Mr. Jones has learned that Luis, an ESOL student with limited formal schooling, had construction experience when he lived in Mexico, and asked Luis if he would talk about his experience with the class.

Luis has agreed, although he admitted to Mr. Jones that he was nervous about speaking to the class because his English skills are not very strong. Mr. Jones encouraged Luis to practice beforehand. "It's fine to gather your ideas in Spanish. Ask your dad for some help too."

Luis brainstorms the ideas he would like to cover in the talk and gets ideas from his father. He decides to practice with his friend Ramón. Luis writes notes for the speech about building a shed in Spanish first. He checks with Mr. Jones about the topics to include and then rewrites his notes in English, being sure to address all the requested topics.

Luis gives the speech to the class 3 days later, and it is well received. Several classmates ask some questions that Luis feels confident answering. When the construction project begins the following day, Luis works with the redecorating and bookshelf-building groups to plan, measure, and estimate costs. He gives advice and applies his prior knowledge to the project at hand.

Discussion

Students are encouraged to

- brainstorm ideas with native language peers prior to writing a composition on a given topic
- practice an oral report with a peer prior to presenting it in class
- verbalize relationships between new information and information previously learned in another setting
- seek more knowledgeable others with whom to consult to advance understanding
- seek out print and nonprint resources in the native language when needed

Mr. Jones' high school consumer math class is composed of students in Grades 9–11, mainly native English speakers with a few nonnative speakers who have beginning English language skills. In this class, the students use English to achieve academically, and Mr. Jones is not specifically trained to work with ESOL students. Nonetheless, he exhibits good judgment when he encourages Luis to gather and plan his information in Spanish before giving the speech in English to the class.

Luis uses several learning strategies as he approaches his task. He uses his native language skills to develop his English language skills. He brainstorms and practices before giving his talk on constructing a shed. By practicing with his friend, he receives feedback in a nonthreatening environment. He also gathers information from a nonprint resource, namely his father, and seeks assistance from Mr. Jones to make sure he understands the assignment and the teacher's expectations. Also important is Luis' ability to connect new and prior knowledge. By drawing from his construction experience in Mexico, he becomes a resource to his classmates as he applies the known information to the new class project.

He encourages Luis to gather and plan his information in Spanish before giving the speech in English to the class.

Grades 9–12

Goal 3, Standard 1

To use English in socially and culturally appropriate ways: Students will use the appropriate language variety, register, and genre according to audience, purpose, and setting

Descriptors

- using the appropriate degree of formality with different audiences and settings

- recognizing and using standard English and vernacular dialects appropriately

- using a variety of writing styles appropriate for different audiences, purposes, and settings

- responding to and using slang appropriately

- responding to and using idioms appropriately

- responding to and using humor appropriately

- determining when it is appropriate to use a language other than English

- determining appropriate topics for interaction

Sample Progress Indicators

- recognize and apply the style of speech used in a job interview, a debate, or a formal meeting

- select topics appropriate to discuss in a job interview

- interpret and explain a political cartoon, situation comedy, or a joke

- recognize irony, sarcasm, and humor in a variety of contexts

- use the appropriate register for business and friendly transactions

- prepare and deliver a short persuasive presentation to different audiences

- write a dialogue incorporating idioms or slang

- write business and personal letters

- create a commercial using an appropriate language style for the product

- create a cartoon or comic book

- initiate and carry on appropriate small talk (e.g., while visiting a classmate's home, on a bus, at a party)

- determine when it is appropriate to tell a joke

- use idiomatic speech appropriately

- advise peers on appropriate language use

- express humor through verbal and non-verbal means

- interact with an adult in a formal and informal setting

- role play a telephone conversation with an adult

- make polite requests

- use English and native languages appropriately in a multilingual social situation (e.g., cooperative games or team sports)

- write a letter or e-mail message to an adult or a peer using appropriate language forms

- demonstrate an understanding of ways to give and receive compliments, show gratitude, apologize, express anger or impatience

- greet and take leave appropriately in a variety of settings

9–12 Vignette

Grade Level:	Ninth grade in a self-contained ESL class
English Proficiency Level:	Intermediate
Language of Instruction:	English
Focus of Instruction:	Language use
Location:	Urban school district in the Southeast

Background

The following vignette describes a ninth-grade, self-contained ESL class in an urban school district, which is taught by Mr. Murray, a bilingual English/Spanish teacher certified in ESL and bilingual education. The class contains 15 intermediate ESOL students from 13 different countries who speak eight different languages. The class has been studying the difference in how language is used according to the context, participants, and topic. To date, the students have made various requests orally and in writing for information from friends, family, teachers, and businesses. Groups of students have videotaped sample transactions at a store in which students had to purchase and return an item and either complain to the manager or compliment the manager as a result of their transaction.

Instructional Sequence

In today's lesson, the students are examining the videotapes of the store transactions. They are working in small cooperative groups and critiquing their own videotaped transaction as well as those of the other group members. Mr. Murray and the class previously created a checklist to provide structure for the critique process. The checklist was developed as a performance assessment tool to review what the students had learned about appropriate behaviors to use when conducting the transaction as well as to guide their viewing of the videotapes after the transactions had been completed. Students have been assigned roles in their groups: One student is the facilitator, another is the note taker, and the third is the videotape production manager. All students play the role of the critiquer.

Alana, the facilitator of Group 1, works to keep her group on task. After they viewed the first videotape and shared their reactions, she asks Frederic to explain what he means when he says that Vladimir did not use the correct form to ask to see the manager. Frederic checks the quote he wrote down while viewing Vladimir's videotape. (The checklist requires him to write down specific quotes in order to critique them.) Frederic reads aloud. "Vladimir said, 'Take me to your manager.' I think he should have been more polite." Mr. Murray overhears the remark and inquires, "What might Vladimir have said?" Frederic pauses and then says, "Maybe he could say 'May I see the manager?'" Alana agrees. Then she adds, "Or, he could say it like a polite sentence, 'I would like to see the manager.'" Nodding, Mr. Murray asks, "Why are those two options better?" Frederic explains, "Well, like, Vladimir didn't have a problem with the manager, you know? If he wants the manager to help him, then he should start by being nice."

Discussion

Students are encouraged to

- ▸ use the appropriate register for business and friendly transactions
- ▸ demonstrate an understanding of ways to give and receive compliments, show gratitude, apologize, express anger or impatience

The ninth-grade class is composed of nonnative speakers of English. In this vignette the students learned how to modify their use of English in various situations. The students were required to purchase something at the store, return it, and then either complain to the manager or compliment the manager on the service they received. In this particular lesson, the students were working in their cooperative learning groups to discuss their critiques of each other's transactions.

Alana, like her classmates, exhibited an intermediate level of proficiency in English yet a high-level proficiency in social skills. She performed very well in her group and worked with other members to accomplish the task at hand. She was skillful at helping the other students in the group learn to support their critiques with specific information, as in a quote or from notes taken during the viewing.

Mr. Murray has created a learning environment where students work together to practice using various forms of English in meaningful, realistic settings, such as the transactions at the store. Not only do students demonstrate their language use in these situations, but also they have an opportunity to review the transactions later and reconsider their choice of register and degree of formality. In small groups, the students make suggestions or give advice for language modifications, always grounding their opinions in the intent of the speaker and setting in which the interaction takes place.

In small groups, the students make suggestions or give advice for language modifications, always grounding their opinions in the intent of the speaker and setting in which the interaction takes place.

Grades 9–12

9–12 Vignette

Grade Level:	Eleventh and twelfth grade in a regular career education class
English Proficiency Level:	Intermediate to advanced
Language of Instruction:	English
Focus of Instruction:	Cosmetology
Location:	Suburban school district in the Midwest

Background

The following vignette describes a cosmetology class with ESOL students mainstreamed among native English speakers. The class is taught by Ms. Crabtree, an English-speaking cosmetology instructor who has no formal training in ESL or second language acquisition. The class of 19 students includes five intermediate- and advanced-level ESOL students from four countries, all of whom speak Spanish as a native language. The class is studying workplace social skills as they apply to working in a team and encountering clients in a cosmetology salon. To date, the students have worked on a variety of academic content-based projects in teams and worked with clients from the local community in the school's cosmetology salon. Topics have included the use of English for communication in the workplace, greeting customers, assessing the customers' desires and needs, and making small talk with them. Students have done written work related to cosmetology and human relations in the past.

Instructional Sequence

At the beginning of class, after all the students are seated, Ms. Crabtree engages in a very brief conversation, greeting a student in the back of the class. She then asks the students to tell her what they recall from the conversation and writes what they tell her in dialogue form on a piece of newsprint. She asks what this form of writing is called, to elicit the word dialogue. She tells the students they will be writing a dialogue in small groups and divides her class into four writing teams. Two teams are seated on opposite sides of the room with all students facing an A-frame easel in the middle of the room. On each side of the easel is a different set of instructions. One set of instructions asks Teams 1 and 2 to write a dialogue in which a customer has a positive communication experience with the salon employees through their use of polite and professional language. Teams 3 and 4 are to write a dialogue in which the customer has a negative experience due to overly casual or improper language or comments by the salon employees. Further directions tell Teams 1 and 3 to write about a new customer entering the salon for the first time and Teams 2 and 4 to write about a regular customer already seated and in the middle of the styling process. Additionally, each team is to make a list of special words, phrases, and topics that are either appropriate or inappropriate in the context of a professional salon. The two teams that work on a positive communication dialogue are instructed to make lists of negative communication attributes, and the other teams make a list of positive attributes.

After the students write the dialogues, each group performs for the class. After each performance, the teacher asks the students to identify the positive or negative language that was used and if the interactions were realistic or exaggerated. In cases of exaggerated behavior, the instructor asks for other words or behaviors that might be more realistic. The language used in the dialogues is compared with the word and topic lists that each team created. After all the dialogues are performed and discussed, the students have an open discussion on the importance of proper language in the salon context.

Discussion

Students are encouraged to

- use the appropriate register for business and friendly transactions
- greet and take leave appropriately in a variety of settings
- initiate and carry on appropriate small talk (e.g., while visiting a classmate's home, on a bus, at a party)
- advise peers on appropriate language use

Ms. Crabtree uses a variety of activities to reinforce the concept that language is used in different ways in different settings. Although this lesson begins by asking students to read directions and write a dialogue (which the teacher models), the fundamental component of the lesson is intended to be oral language as used in a professional context. Students in her cosmetology class have an opportunity to conceive of a potential conversation with a customer and act it out for the class. The dialogue instructions direct the teams to consider not only different customers—one with whom the hair stylist is very familiar and one who is a new customer, but also the type of oral interaction that might occur at different points during the styling transaction (e.g., greetings, requesting information, small talk). The students work in a group to do this, gaining practice in that important workplace skill.

Classmates are asked to comment on the dialogue presentations and discuss negative and positive attributes of the interaction. Because the dialogues may only focus on one negative or positive topic or a limited set of appropriate or inappropriate words, Ms. Crabtree broadens the students' awareness through the list activity. Through this process and with teacher input, the students identify appropriate language and topics for use with customers in a salon.

Goal 3, Standard 2

To use English in socially and culturally appropriate ways: Students will use nonverbal communication appropriate to audience, purpose, and setting

Descriptors

- interpreting and responding appropriately to nonverbal cues and body language
- demonstrating knowledge of acceptable nonverbal classroom behaviors
- using acceptable tone, volume, stress, and intonation, in various social settings*
- recognizing and adjusting behavior in response to nonverbal cues

Sample Progress Indicators

- compare body language norms among various cultures represented in the classroom or community
- compare gestures and body language acceptable in formal and informal settings
- identify nonverbal cues that cause misunderstanding
- advise peers on appropriate behaviors in and out of school
- determine the appropriate distance to maintain while standing near someone, depending on the situation
- maintain appropriate level of eye contact with audience while giving an oral presentation
- demonstrate in a role play two aspects of body language common to one's own culture
- analyze nonverbal behavior
- describe intent by focusing on a person's nonverbal behavior
- add gestures to correspond to a dialogue in a play
- respond appropriately to a teacher's gesture
- obtain a teacher's attention in an appropriate manner
- use appropriate volume of voice in different settings such as the library, hall, gymnasium, supermarket, and movie theater

* For the purposes of this standard, TESOL considers tone, volume, stress, and intonation as part of nonverbal communication, along with physical manifestations of communication, such as gestures and proxemics.

Grades 9–12

9–12 Vignette

Grade Level: Tenth grade in a social studies class
English Proficiency Level: Intermediate to advanced
Language of Instruction: English
Focus of Instruction: Social studies
Location: Suburban school district in the West

Background

The following vignette describes a social studies class where half of the students have a native language other than English. Students come from Mexico, China, Palestine, and Russia. Three out of those 10 students have nativelike proficiency in English while the rest are at an intermediate level. The rest of the students are native speakers of English from the mainstream culture. The teacher, Ms. Bohland, who has had ESOL students for 6 years, has taken two graduate-level courses on teaching linguistically and culturally diverse students.

Instructional Sequence

The class is completing a unit in sociology. In this lesson, Ms. Bohland steers the discussion to focus on the issue of formality, and she shows a short clip from a Marx Brothers movie in which the protagonists attend a very formal event and act in extremely inappropriate ways. The clip is shown without sound, so that students can focus on the nonverbal aspects of behavior. The students then make a list of the inappropriate behaviors they observed in small, mixed-ability groups and the entire class discusses how they would change those behaviors to be more appropriate for the context. Using that list, the groups create a Venn Diagram to compare behaviors in formal and informal settings. If inappropriate behaviors from the list might suit informal settings, the students add them to that section of the diagram. If the behaviors do not fit anywhere, the students write them around the outside of the Venn circles. The groups then complete the diagram with other appropriate behaviors. While the groups work, Ms. Bohland makes a list of some of the vocabulary that was new to the ESOL students to give to the ESL tutor who works with the students after school 3 days a week.

After the groups share their diagrams, Ms. Bohland focuses on customs that groups or communities share. She elicits from the ESOL students ways in which customs differ in the various cultures they represent. For homework, the students are asked to interview an older person from their own culture and have them talk about some of the differences in nonverbal aspects of interaction that they have experienced with someone from a different culture. The next day, students will present their findings.

Discussion

Students are encouraged to

- compare body language norms among various cultures represented in the classroom or community
- compare gestures and body language acceptable in formal and informal settings
- analyze nonverbal behavior

This lesson takes place in a diverse, mainstream classroom. Although the curriculum is not sheltered, Ms. Bohland makes accommodations for the ESOL students, namely by using mixed ability groups, multimedia, graphic organizers, and targeted vocabulary learning. The after-school tutor provides additional support for these language learners.

The movie clip is an excellent prompt for a discussion of appropriate behaviors in formal and informal settings. By beginning with a movie, the students can analyze behavior in a non-threatening way. In small groups, they have more opportunities to use English as they discuss what they saw and complete the assigned task. Later, Ms. Bohland builds on the one culture reflected in the movie by expanding the discovery to embrace many cultures. She asks all the students to explore nonverbal communication across cultures, seeking information from the local community. The students will use English to gather the information and report it back to the class.

Ms. Bohland makes accommodations for the ESOL students, namely by using mixed ability groups, multimedia, graphic organizers, and targeted vocabulary learning.

Grades 9–12

Goal 3, Standard 3

To use English in socially and culturally appropriate ways:
Students will use appropriate learning strategies to extend their
communicative competence

Descriptors

- observing and modeling how others speak and behave in a particular situation or setting
- experimenting with variations of language in social and academic settings
- seeking information about appropriate language use and behavior
- self-monitoring and self-evaluating language use according to setting and audience
- analyzing the social context to determine appropriate language use
- rehearsing variations for language in different social and academic settings
- deciding when use of slang is appropriate

Sample Progress Indicators

- evaluate different types of communication for effectiveness in making one's point
- interpret meaning through knowledge of cultural factors that affect meaning (e.g., word choice, intonation, setting)
- model behavior and language use of others in different situations and settings
- rephrase an utterance when it results in cultural misunderstanding
- evaluate behaviors in different situations
- observe language use and behaviors of peers in different settings
- rehearse different ways of speaking according to the formality of the setting
- test appropriate use of newly acquired gestures and language

Grades 9–12

9–12 Vignette

Grade Level:	Twelfth grade in an internship program
English Proficiency Level:	Intermediate
Language of Instruction:	English
Focus of Instruction:	Workplace skills
Location:	Urban school district in the East

Background

The following vignette describes students in a career internship program where each student spends 4 days per week for one semester in one of a variety of community workplaces. These include schools, factories, businesses, hospitals, and so forth. The program is coordinated by the school-to-work counselor. All students in the school participate in the program and because of the large number of ESOL students, one of the bilingual teachers consults with the counselor. This vignette describes the activities of several ESOL and native-English-speaking students who will complete their internship in the local hospital.

Instructional Sequence

In early December, Mr. Castellano, the bilingual teacher, suggests to Mrs. Reinhardt, the school-to-work counselor, that the students in the bilingual program who will be participating in the second semester internship prepare for the activity in advance, through a mini-research project on language use in the workplace. Mrs. Reinhardt welcomes the idea because several of her nonnative English speaking students have, in the past, commented that they were not always able to communicate well with their co-workers. Mrs. Reinhardt realizes that this activity would benefit native-English-speaking students as well. The two teachers agree to have all the second-semester students observe and interview their peers currently at the worksites.

Mr. Castellano gets the students together after school to prepare them for the language observations. First, he calls upon the students to share any experiences they have had where communication has been difficult. After a few students discuss miscommunication with their parents or boyfriends and girlfriends, Mr. Castellano guides the discussion toward communication in the workplace. He explains there are norms and customs for communication in work environments that might be unfamiliar to those outside that work site. At this point, he describes the research assignment and asks the students to work in small groups and generate a list of scenarios where different types of language might be used in the workplace. Students suggest the lunchroom, the boss' office, the place where a worker interacts with a customer, and so on. As a whole group, they decide what to look for: Who initiates conversations? Who does most of the talking? What topics are used? How formal is the language? What is the role of humor? Is it okay to use a language other than English at work?

Each second-semester student is paired with a current internship student and spends two days shadowing that person "on the job." Verónica follows Amelia, another student from the bilingual program, as she works around the hospital linen supply room. Verónica jots down notes about specific interaction styles and language patterns that she notices and, at the end of the first day, consults with Amelia about certain things she does not understand. For example, she asks Amelia whether she realizes that she speaks differently to the drivers who bring the fresh linen each morning and the nurse managers who pop in from time to time. Amelia reflects on this and comes to the realization that she does adjust her speech according to her conversation partner.

The next day, when a nurse comes by to complain that sheet supplies are low on her floor, Amelia is very brusque with her and continues piling the blankets on the shelf. After the nurse leaves in a huff, Verónica points out that Amelia may have upset the nurse by being inappropriately abrupt and not seeming to care. Although Amelia agrees, she cannot come up with an appropriate response that she could have given the nurse. The two discuss this and then think of some different options. Verónica writes them down and promises to take them back to school the following day to get some feedback from Mr. Castellano.

Discussion

Students are encouraged to

- evaluate different types of communication for effectiveness in making one's point
- evaluate behaviors in different situations
- observe language use and behaviors of peers in different settings
- test appropriate use of newly acquired gestures and language

In this vignette, the bilingual teacher was well aware of the need to develop language observation skills in his students so that they might continue to learn to use language in appropriate ways. This is a skill that even native speakers of English would benefit from, both to become more effective speakers and listeners and to develop an awareness of language norms. Mrs. Reinhardt concurs when Mr. Castellano brings it to her attention. She makes it possible for him to work with not only the bilingual students but the native English speakers as well.

In the school setting, students talk about language use at work and prepare to investigate it. At the hospital, Verónica evaluates the appropriateness and effectiveness of different ways of speaking with Amelia as they discuss the observations that Verónica has made while watching Amelia work. This activity is not threatening to Amelia; rather it allows her to think about language use herself. Furthermore, because the students have had practice in giving advice to peers through writing workshops in class with Mr. Castellano, the two girls are able to communicate well. Through their conversations, Verónica and Amelia both increase their self-awareness of language use on the job. After a negative communication experience occurs, Verónica and Amelia consider alternative language that might have resulted in a more positive outcome. Verónica chooses to check the appropriateness of their suggestions the Mr. Castellano.

Grades 9–12

Glossary

academic language: language used in the learning of academic subject matter in formal schooling context; aspects of language strongly associated with literacy and academic achievement, including specific academic terms or technical language, and speech registers related to each field of study

additive bilingualism: a process by which individuals develop proficiency in a second language subsequent to or simultaneous with the development of proficiency in the primary language, without loss of the primary language; a bilingual situation where the addition of a second language and culture are unlikely to replace or displace the first language and culture

assessment standards: statements that establish guidelines for evaluating student performance and attainment of content standards; often include philosophical statements of good assessment practice (see *performance standards*)

authentic language: real or natural language, as used by native speakers of a language in real-life contexts; not artificial or contrived for purposes of learning grammatical forms or vocabulary

biculturalism: near nativelike knowledge of two cultures; includes the ability to respond effectively to the different demands of these two cultures

bilingual instruction: provision of instruction in school settings through the medium of two languages, usually a native and a second language; the proportion of the instructional day delivered in each language varies by the type of the bilingual education program in which instruction is offered and the goals of said program

body language: the gestures and mannerisms by which a person communicates with others

communicative competence: the ability to recognize and to produce authentic and appropriate language correctly and fluently in any situation; use of language in realistic, everyday settings; involves grammatical competence, sociolinguistic competence, discourse competence, and strategic competence

communicative functions: purposes for which language is used; includes three broad functions: communicative, integrative, and expressive; where language aids the transmission of information, aids affiliation and belonging to a particular social group, and allows the display of individual feelings, ideas, and personality

comprehensible input: a construct developed to describe understandable and meaningful language directed at second language learners under optimal conditions; it is characterized as the language the learner already knows plus a range of new language that is made comprehensible by the use of certain planned strategies (e.g., use of concrete referents)

content-based ESL: a model of language education that integrates language and content instruction in the second language classroom; a second language learning approach where second language teachers use instructional materials, learning tasks, and classroom techniques from academic content areas as the vehicle for developing second language, content, cognitive and study skills

content standards: statements that define what one is expected to know and be able to do in a content area; the knowledge, skills, processes, and other understandings that schools should teach in order for students to attain high levels of competency in challenging subject matter; the subject-specific knowledge, processes, and skills that schools are expected to teach and students are expected to learn

cooperative/collaborative group: a grouping arrangement in which positive interdependence and shared responsibility for task completion are established among group members; the type of organizational structure encouraging heterogeneous grouping, shared leadership, and social skills development

cross-cultural competence: ability to function according to the cultural rules of more than one cultural system; ability to respond in culturally sensitive and appropriate ways according to the cultural demands of a given situation

culture: the sum total of the ways of life of a people; includes norms, learned behavior patterns, attitudes, and artifacts; also involves traditions, habits or customs; how people behave, feel and interact; the means by which they order and interpret the world; ways of perceiving, relating and interpreting events based on established social norms; a system of standards for perceiving, believing, evaluating, and acting

descriptors: broad categories of discrete, representative behaviors that students exhibit when they meet a standard

dialect: a regional or social variety of language distinguished by features of vocabulary, grammar, pronunciation, and discourse that differ from other varieties

ESL: the field of English as a second language; courses, classes and/or programs designed for students learning English as an additional language

ESOL student: English to speakers of other languages; refers to learners who are identified as still in the process of acquiring English as an additional language; students who may not speak English at all or, at least, do not speak, understand, and write English with the same facility as their classmates because they did not grow up speaking English (rather they primarily spoke another language at home)

genre: a category of literary composition characterized by a particular style, form, or content (e.g., an historical novel is one fictional genre)

home language: language(s) spoken in the home by significant others (e.g., family members, caregivers) who reside in the child's home; sometimes used as a synonym for first language, primary language, or native language

idiom: an expression in the usage of a language that has a meaning that cannot be derived from the conjoined meanings of its elements (e.g., *raining cats and dogs*)

language "chunks": short phrases learned as a unit (e.g., *thank you very much*); patterned language acquired through redundant use, such as refrains and repetitive phrases in stories

language minority: a student who comes from a home in which a language other than English is primarily spoken; the student may or may not speak English well

language proficiency: the level of competence at which an individual is able to use language for both basic communicative tasks and academic purposes

language variety: variations of a language used by particular groups of people, includes regional dialects characterized by distinct vocabularies, speech patterns, grammatical features, and so forth; may also vary by social group (sociolect) or idiosyncratically for a particular individual (idiolect)

learning strategies: mental activities or actions that assist in enhancing learning outcomes; may include metacognitive strategies (e.g., planning for learning, monitoring one's own comprehension and production, evaluating one's performance); cognitive strategies (e.g., mental or physical manipulation of the material), or social/affective strategies (e.g., interacting with another person to assist learning, using self-talk to persist at a difficult task until resolution)

linguistic competence: a broad term used to describe the totality of a given individual's language ability; the underlying language system believed to exist as inferred from an individual's language performance

multilingualism: ability to speak more than two languages; proficiency in many languages

native language: primary or first language spoken by an individual

nonverbal communication: paralinguistic and nonlinguistic messages that can be transmitted in conjunction with language or without the aid of language; paralinguistic mechanisms include intonation, stress, rate of speech, and pauses or hesitations; nonlinguistic behaviors include gestures, facial expressions, and body language, among others

performance standards: statements that refer to how well students are meeting a content standard; specify the quality and effect of student performance at various levels of competency (benchmarks) in the subject matter; specify how students must demonstrate their knowledge and skills and can show student progress toward meeting a standard

primary language: first or native language spoken by an individual

progress indicators: assessable, observable activities that students may perform to show progress toward meeting the standard; organized by grade-level clusters

proxemics: the study of distances maintained by speakers of different languages as they speak to each other or others

proximity norms: cultural behaviors associated with the distance and body positioning maintained by members of the same culture during conversation

pull-out instruction: in the case of ESL pull-out instruction, when students are withdrawn from their regular classrooms for one or more periods a week for special classes of ESL instruction in small groups

realia: concrete objects used to relate classroom teaching to real life (e.g., use of actual foods and supermarket circulars to develop the language related to foods, food purchasing)

register: usage of different varieties of language, depending on the setting, the relationship among the individuals involved in the communication, and the function of the interaction; a form of a language that is appropriate to the social or functional context

regular class: as used in this document, refers to a class with or without ESOL students that does not systematically accommodate the language learning needs of ESOL students. May be a regular elementary class or a subject area class at a secondary level where all instruction is delivered and materials are provided almost exclusively in English; sometimes referred to as a mainstream class

self-contained ESL class: typically an ESL class with only ESOL students; all subject matter taught to ESOL students by their ESL classroom teacher and no pull-out ESL instruction used

sheltered instruction: an approach in which students develop knowledge in specific subject areas through the medium of English, their second language; teachers adjust the language demands of the lesson in many ways, such as modifying speech rate and tone, using context clues and models extensively, relating instruction to student experience, adapting the language of texts or tasks, and using certain methods familiar to language teachers (e.g., demonstrations, visuals, graphic organizers, or cooperative work) to make academic instruction more accessible to students of different English proficiency levels

social functions: use of language to accomplish various purposes, such as asking for or giving information, describing past actions, expressing feelings, and expressing regret

social language: the aspects of language proficiency strongly associated with basic fluency in face-to-face-interaction; natural speech in social interactions, including those that occur in a classroom

sociocultural competence: ability to function effectively in a particular social or cultural context according to the rules or expectancies for behavior held by members of that social or cultural group

sociolinguistic competence: related to communicative competence; the extent to which language is appropriately understood and used in a given situation (e.g., the ability to make apologies, give compliments, and politely refuse requests)

subtractive bilingualism: the learning of a majority language at the expense of the first; refers to cases where the first language and culture have low status and where because of this, learners are encouraged to divest themselves of their first language and culture and to replace them with the second language and culture; primary language attrition or loss and cultural anomie (uncertainty, alienation) often result from a subtractive bilingual situation

two-way bilingual immersion program: a program in which monolingual English-speaking children study the regular school curriculum alongside children who are native speakers of the target, or second, language; a portion of the instructional day is taught in English and another portion is in the target language; aims for additive bilingualism and biculturalism for all the students involved

vernacular: language or dialect native to a region or country; normal spoken form of a language; includes nonstandard dialects

Sources of Definitions Used in Glossary

Baker, C. (1993). *Foundations of bilingual education and bilingualism*. Clevedon, England: Multilingual Matters.

Canale, M., & Swain, M. (1980). Theoretical bases of communicative approaches to second language teaching and testing. *Applied Linguistics, 1*, 1-47.

Chamot, A.U., & O'Malley, J.M. (1994). *The CALLA handbook: Implementing the cognitive academic language learning approach*. Reading, MA: Addison-Wesley.

Crandall, J. (1994). Content-centered language learning. *ERIC Digest*. Washington, DC: ERIC Clearinghouse on Languages and Linguistics, Center for Applied Linguistics.

Lessow-Hurley, J. (1990). *The foundations of dual language instruction*. White Plains, NY: Longman.

Prince, C.D., & Forgione, P.D. (1993). Raising standards and measuring performance equitably: Challenges for the National Education Goals Panel and state assessment systems. In G. Burkart (Ed.), *Goal three: The issues of language and culture* (pp. 11-22). Washington, DC: Center for Applied Linguistics.

Office of Bilingual Bicultural Education, California State Department of Education. (1981). *Schooling and language minority students: A theoretical framework*. Los Angeles, CA: Evaluation, Dissemination and Assessment Center, California State University, Los Angeles.

Scarcella, R. (1990). *Teaching language minority students in the multicultural classroom*. Englewood Cliffs, NJ: Prentice-Hall.

Schumann, J. (1978). *The pidginization process: A model for second language acquisition*. Rowley, MA: Newbury House.

Snow, M.A., Met, M., & Genesee, F. (1989). A conceptual framework for the integration of language and content in second/foreign language instruction. *TESOL Quarterly, 23*(2), 201-217.

Struggling for standards. (1995, April 12). *Education Week*, p. 8.

Watson, D.L., Northcutt, L., & Rydell, L. (1989). Teaching bilingual students successfully. *Educational Leadership, 46*, 59-61.

Webster's ninth new collegiate dictionary. (1988). Springfield, MA: Merriam-Webster.

Zehler, A.M. (1994). *Working with English language learners: Strategies for elementary and middle school teachers* (Program Information Guide No. 19). Washington, DC: National Clearinghouse for Bilingual Education.

Appendix A:

Access Brochure

The TESOL Standards
Ensuring Access to Quality Educational Experiences for Language Minority Students

Language minority students are those students who learned a language other than English as their first language. These students may be immigrants, refugees, or native born Americans. They may come to school with extensive formal education or they may be academically delayed or illiterate in their first language. Such students arrive at school with varying degrees of English proficiency. Some may not speak English at all; others may speak English, but need assistance in reading or writing English.

Whatever the case, it is clear that schools that hope to help these students meet the National Education Goals must provide special assistance to them. While the type of special assistance may vary from one district or school to another, all special assistance programs must give language minority students full access to the learning environment, the curriculum, special services and assessment in a meaningful way.

Teachers of English to Speakers of Other Languages, Inc. (TESOL) offers the following standards of access to help schools judge the degree to which programs of special assistance are helping language minority students to meet the National Education Goals. The standards have been developed by the TESOL Task Force on the Education of Language Minority Students, K–12, in the United States. They are based on the most current research on language learning in academic settings.

Access to a Positive Learning Environment

1. Are the schools attended by language minority students safe, attractive, and free of prejudice?

2. Is there evidence of a positive whole-school environment whose administrative and instructional policies and practices create a climate that is characterized by high expectations as well as linguistically and culturally appropriate learning experiences for language minority students?

3. Are teachers, administrators, and other staff specifically prepared to tailor instructional and other services to the needs of language minority students?

4. Does the school environment welcome and encourage parents of language minority students as at-home primary teachers of their children and as partners in the life of the school? Does the school inform and educate parents and others concerned with the education of language minority students? Does the school systematically and regularly seek input from parents on information and decisions that affect all critical aspects of the education of language minority students, their schools and school districts?

Access to Appropriate Curriculum

5. Do language minority students have access to special instructional programs that support the second language development necessary to participate in the full range of instructional services offered to majority students?

6. Does the core curriculum designed for all students include those aspects that promote (a) the sharing, valuing, and development of both first and second languages and cultures among all students and (b) the higher order thinking skills required for learning across the curriculum?

7. Do language minority students have access to the instructional programs and related services that identify, conduct and support programs for special populations in a district? Such programs include, but are not limited to, early childhood programs, special education programs, and gifted and talented programs, as well as programs for students with handicapping conditions or disabilities, migrant education programs, programs for recent immigrants, and programs designed for students with low levels of literacy or mathematical skills, such as Chapter 1.*

Access to Full Delivery of Services

8. Are the teaching strategies and instructional practices used with language minority students developmentally appropriate, attuned to students' language proficiencies and cognitive levels, and culturally supportive and relevant?

9. Do students have opportunities to develop and use their first language to promote academic and social development?

10. Are nonclassroom services and support services (such as counseling, career guidance, and transportation) available to language minority students?

11. Do language minority students have equal access to computers, computer classes and other technologically advanced instructional assistance?

12. Does the school have institutional policies and procedures that are linguistically and culturally sensitive to the particular needs of language minority students and their communities?

---

* Chapter 1 is now referred to as Title 1 according to the reauthorized Elementary and Secondary Education Act of 1995.

13. Does the school offer regular, nonstereotypical opportunities for native-English-speaking students and language minority students to share and value one another's languages and cultures?

Access to Equitable Assessment

14. Do language minority students have access to broadly based methods of assessing language and academic achievement in the content areas that are appropriate to students' developmental level, age, and level of oral and written language proficiency in the first and second languages? Are these measures nonbiased and relevant? Are the results of such assessments explained to the community from which the student comes in the language which that community uses?

15. Do language minority students have access to broadly based methods of assessing special needs? Again, access is further defined by using measures that are nonbiased and relevant, the results of which are explained to the community from which the student comes and in the language which that community uses.

Appendix B:

Committee and Writing Team Members, Reviewers, and Production Staff

TESOL ESL Standards Project Committee Members

Nancy Cloud, Hofstra University
Emily Gómez, Center for Applied Linguistics
Else Hamayan, Illinois Resource Center
Sarah Hudelson, Arizona State University
Jean Ramirez, San Francisco Unified School
    District
Deborah Short, Center for Applied Linguistics

Assessment Writing Team

Fred Genesee, University of California at
    Davis
Margo Gottleib, Illinois Resource Center
Anne Katz (Chair), ARC Associates
Meg Malone, U.S. Peace Corps

TESOL Board Liaisons

Fred Genesee, University of California at
    Davis
Natalie Kuhlman, San Diego State University
Denise Murray, San José State University

TESOL Executive Director

Susan Bayley

TESOL Central Office

Brandi Berry
Carol Epps
Ann Kammerer
Helen Kornblum
Marilyn Kupetz
Ellison Loth
Terry O'Donnell
Lisa Queeney
Tina Ringling
Robert Ward

Past Task Force Chairs

Denise McKeon, AERA
Else Hamayan, IRC

Alaska Writing Team (AKABE)

Toby Allen, Anchorage, AK
Bobbie Bitters, Fairbanks, AK
LaVonne Bridges, Anchorage, AK
*Janice Jones Schroeder, Anch., AK
Alicia Martinez, Anchorage, AK
David Olivera, Anchorage, AK
Molli Sipe, Fairbanks, AK
Jeff Troiano, Anchorage, AK
Karen Walters, Atmautlauk, AK
Bev Williams, Bethel, AK

*Writing team leader

BATESOL Writing Team

*Carol Bartley, Columbia, MD
Diana Gough, Laurel, MD
Beth Stiefel-Itoh, Owings Mills, MD

CATESOL Writing Team

Pre-K–3 Team
*Sara Fields, Culver City, CA
Becky Rockwood, Vista, CA
Charlene Ruble, Orange, CA

4–8 Team
Barbara Thornbury, Monterey, CA
Charlene Zawicki, Escondido, CA

9–12 Team
Linda Sasser, Altadena, CA
Roger Winn-Bell Olsen, San Francisco, CA

COTESOL Writing Team

Nina Amabile, Boulder, CO
Patsy Jaynes, Lakewood, CO
Marsha Knueven, Lakewood, CO
*Barbara Werner, Boulder, CO

Delaware Writing Team

Ariadna Clare, Wyoming, DE
*Linda Cooper-Duncan, Wyoming, DE
Rebecca Scarborough, Dover, DE

FLATESOL Writing Team

*Nilda Aguirre, Plantation, FL
Janet Lecalleet, Key Largo, FL
Lisa Taylor, Key Largo, FL

GATESOL Writing Team

*Susan M. Burke, Atlanta, GA
Judy Schilling, Norcross, GA
Patsy Thompson, Lithonia, GA
Cheryl Wienges, Snellville, GA

MATSOL Writing Team

*Paula Merchant, Canton, MA
Ruth Ann Weinstein, Belmont, MA

Mid-TESOL Writing Team

Susan Hanan, St. Louis, MO
Ella Jean Keeney, Van Buren, MO
*Adelaide Parsons, Cape Girard., MO
Susan Schindler, St. Louis, MO

Montana Writing Team

Angela Branz-Spall, Helena, MT
Mick Fedullo, Pryor, MT
*Lynn Hinch, Helena, MT
Sharon Peregoy, Crow Agency, MT

NJ TESOL Writing Team

Pre-K–3 Team
*Betí Leone, Hawthorne, NJ
Mark Quiles, Hawthorne, NJ
Mary Beth Raymar, Lincoln Park, NJ

4–8 Team
René Cisneros, Hawthorne, NJ
Lisa Baldonado, Valley Cottage, NY
Lorraine Ragone, Passaic, NJ

9–12 Team
Pat Bruce, Westfield, NJ
Carol Campell, Fanwood, NJ
Charlotte Kantz, Westfield, NJ
Leona Marsh, New York, NY
Manuel Menéndez, New York, NY
Helen Shore, Scotch Plains, NJ

*Writing team leader

NYS TESOL Writing Team

*Linda New Levine, Lake Katonah, NY

Pre-K–3 Team

Duane Diviney, Ithaca, NY
Ann Furman, Trumansburg, NY
Alison Williams, Port Jefferson, NY

4–8 Team

Virginia Jama, Jamaica, NY
Carole Kaye, New York, NY
Phyllis Ziegler, New York, NY

9–12 Team

Anthony DeFazio, New York, NY
Nancy Dunetz, Bronx, NY

OHIO TESOL Writing Team

Sachiko Berardi, Columbus, OH
Joan Chryst, Powell, OH
Bea Fishman, Dublin, OH
Maria Hernandez, Dublin, OH
*Elana Hohl, Columbus, OH
Ann Wilder, Columbus, OH

OKTESOL Writing Team

Van Anderson, Oklahoma City, OK
Kathy Burne, Clinton, OK
Lynore Carnuccio, Mustang, OK
Helen Casey, Oklahoma City, OK
Judith LeBlanc Flores, Oklahoma City, OK
April Haulman, Edmond, OK
*Cheryl Huffman, Oklahoma City, OK
JoAnn Webster, Midwest City, OK

Penn TESOL East Writing Team

Pre-K–3 Team

Tomás Hanna, Philadelphia, PA
Robin Marks, Philadelphia, PA
Ruth Montalvo, Philadelphia, PA
Maria Monrás-Sender, Wyncote, PA
Vilma Rivera, Philadelphia, PA

4–8 Team

Maria Beckert, Huntingdon Valley, PA
Richard W. Fairchild, Philadelphia, PA
Cynthia Gross Alvarez, Philadelphia, PA
Howard Heicklen, Horsham, PA
*Mary I. Ramirez, Philadelphia, PA
Diana Regan, Bryn Mawr, PA

Rhode Island Writing Team

Gerardine Cannon, Pawtucket, RI
Roberta Costa, Cranston, RI
Ellen Hedlund, Providence, RI
Barbara Jamieson, Cranston, RI
*Maria Lindia, Providence, RI
Maria Mansella, North Providence, RI
Rosemary Powers, Cranston, RI
Iva de Silva, Pawtucket, RI

WATESOL Writing Team

Patricia Boukeroui, Bethesda, MD
Emily Gómez, Arlington, VA
Stephen Lewis, Alexandria, VA
Grace Rissetto, Falls Church, VA
Cindy Ross, Sterling, VA
*Roberta Schlicher, Arlington, VA
Rich Spence, Burke, VA

WITESOL Writing Team

Linda Jenks

*Writing team leader

Key Advisors and Invited Reviewers

Susan Andrews
Dennis W. Cheek
Nancy Clair
Virginia Collier
Rosa Castro Feinberg
Sandra H. Fradd
Erminda García
Kenji Hakuta
Michele Hewlett-Gómez
Suzanne Irujo
Jack Jennings
Betí Leone
Linda New Levine
Janice Marcin
Amy Mazur
Denise McKeon
Rebecca Moscosco
J. Michael O'Malley
J. E. Olsen
Roger Winn-Bell Olsen
Susan J. Parks
Lise Ragan
Terry Salinger

Rebecca Scarborough
Roberta Schlicher
Carmen Simich-Dudgeon
Karen Smith
Jim Stack
Rita LaNell Stahl
Dean Stecker
Carlyn Syvanen
G. Richard Tucker
Laurie Wellman
Lily Wong Fillmore
Nancy Zelasko

Graphic Design Advisors

Jimmy Nelle, San Francisco, CA
Vincent Sagart, Silver Spring, MD

Production Assistants

Margaret Crandall, Center for Applied
    Linguistics
Annette Holmes, Center for Applied
    Linguistics
Sonia Kundert, Center for Applied Linguistics